Ever Remember

Ever Remember
The Days of 1913–1914

John Pearce

State House Press
Buffalo Gap, Texas

Library of Congress Cataloging-in-Publication Data

Pearce, John
Ever Remember The Days of 1913–1914
John Pearce
Includes Bibliographical references and index.
ISBN 978-1-933337-61-6 (pbk. alk. paper)
ISBN- 933337-61-3 (pbk. alk. paper)
1. History United States 2. History / Texas 3. United States: History-20th century. 4. Texas History / East Texas. 5. Memoir, Alma Caldwell, Sulphur Springs, Texas
This paper meets the requirements of ANSI/NISO, Z39.48-1992 (permanence of paper) Binding materials have been chosen for durability
I. Title.
"Cataloging-in-Publication Data available from the Library of Congress"

Manufactured in the United States

First Edition

State House Press
P.O. Box 818
Buffalo Gap, Texas 79508
325-572-3974 · 325-572-3991 (fax)
www.tfhcc.com

Printed in the United States of America
Distributed by Texas A&M University Press Consortium
800-826-8911
www.tamupress.com

ISBN-13: 978-1-933337-61-6
ISBN-10: 1-933337-61-3

Book Design by Rosenbohm Graphic Design

To my wife Jaime and daughter Amy for their loving support—without them this story would have been lost in history.

Contents

Acknowledgments

It is humbling when I realized how many people were instrumental in the writing, researching, editing, and printing of *Ever Remember*.

To State House Press of the McWhiney History Education Group, thank you for making this a dream come true. Especially, a warm thanks to Scott Clowdus, Chief Operating Officer, and Dr. Donald S. Frazier, President and Chief Executive Officer, for accepting and promoting this project.

To project manager for State House Press, Claudia Gravier Frigo, a tireless editor, whose work made the flow of *Ever Remember* easy to grasp and enjoy.

To the Hopkins County Genealogical Society, and notably Marynell Bryant, who made available and aided with the research concerning this book.

To all the Caldwell and Thornton family members, especially Bill Dozier Thornton and Martha Lou Thornton Hughes, for the detailed family information they uncovered and provided.

To my daughter Amy and her family and my son Mike and his family for their positive support in helping me start and finish *Ever Remember*. Without Amy, who discovered Alma Caldwell's diary minutes before it was to be destroyed, Alma's wonder year of 1913–1914 would have been lost.

Finally to the love of my life, my wife Jaime. For more than forty-five years she has been the guiding light for our family. She has never shone brighter than in her belief and encouragement that a retired football coach could successfully write about something other than just *X*'s and *O*'s.

Introduction

Alma Caldwell's diary provides a detailed view of 1913 and 1914. It starts in the summer of 1913 when activities for young people, because of the warm weather, were abundant. Caldwell reluctantly chronicles her return to high school for a junior year, hurdles through the heartbreak of a chilling winter, and rockets full blast into the spring and early summer of 1914. The first chapter introduces Alma and her new boyfriend, Emmet Thornton and the last chapter ends with how their lives played out. In between those chapters is a first-person narrative of the intervening time.

Articles from two newspapers, which covered the two northeast Texas towns she frequented, Sulphur Springs and Commerce, are interspersed through her diary entries. The *Sulphur Springs Gazette* (1862–1928) and *The Commerce Journal* (1891–present) provide more details of some of the events she witnessed. Finally, she kept a notebook of magazine clippings during the time of the diary, which illustrate special moments in her life.

This is the story of a teenager taking a pencil and writing of love, disappointment, secrets never to be revealed, and joy in a time of silent movies, Model T Fords, passenger train rides, and the heartbeat of American entertainment, which was seen under a tent and not on TV—the Chautauqua and Lyceum Courses.

Prelude

Ever remember this year. It has been one of the happiest years I ever spent. I hope every <u>year</u> of my life will always be spent and enjoyed as this one has been.

My <u>school</u> days of 1913 and 14 were so <u>happy</u>—to me. Everything I have written in this Diary is the truth, nothing but the truth.

If this little <u>book</u> should ever stray away, please return it to—

Alma Caldwell

Sulphur Springs, Tex.

Age—16 yrs.

"My first love" <u>Romance</u>

1

Alma and Emmet

"the sweet strains of the violin were heard and soon the spacious hall was a scene of merriment indescribable"

It was a year—a single blissful year—like no other. As one observing the surrounding joys of life in the small northeast Texas town of Sulphur Springs, the June-to-June memoirs of Alma Caldwell and her eventual romance with Emmet Thornton slowly dance through the time period in such a youthful and graceful way. Little did Alma know that it was the end of simplicity in her generation's seemingly carefree world. When she laid aside her pencil in June 1914, it was just days before the destinies of Americans escalated toward the horrors of "The Great War." It became a conflict, which eventually claimed the lives of thousands of US soldiers in Europe, including several enthusiastic young men living in Hopkins County with her.

Alma was raised in one of the most picturesque communities in the state of Texas; as E. B. Fleming noted in the Introduction to his *Early History of Hopkins County*, "[Sulphur Springs was] beautifully situated on the divide between the timber lands and prairie lands, with a good supply of wood and water for all purposes." In 1913, Sulphur Springs showcased the envy of many a neighboring town: an $85,000 limestone courthouse, which dominated the northeastern side of the spacious town square. It featured traveled but well-maintained dirt streets,[1] a sound

1 Just this June, the *Sulphur Springs Gazette* reported "If you want to see one of the best pieces of street improvement that has ever been done in Sulphur Springs just take a ride down Main Street. This street was once the sandiest in the city, and the constant dread of those who had to travel it. Street Commissioner Patrick has clayed it almost to the Sour Well, and it is now one of the best streets in town. Mr. Patrick is also doing splendid work on other streets, cleaning them up and having them graded and drug. He is enthusiastic on street and sidewalk improvements," (*Sulphur Springs Gazette*, June 20, 1913).

Sulphur Springs town square

economy with three banks, the services of seven physicians and surgeons, twelve lawyers, four dentists, a great educational program with a modern high school, and three ward school buildings, all brick, and moderately new, and the newest craze sweeping the nation, movie theater houses.

On the surface, Sulphur Springs was clearly the pride of Hopkins County. However, beneath this personification of perfection, there were cracks in the faultless foundation of the city. The town was divided into two sections—one for the white majority and the other for a small black minority. Cornered in an area known as "East End," the black citizens kept to themselves and accepted their position with only limited debate. The majority of this acceptance was the result of two horrific events orchestrated to keep each social group in their intended place.

Less than eight years before the start of Alma's diary, a black man who attempted to rape a white girl just west of Sulphur Springs was physically taken from law officers by an angry mob of locals. He was shot, set on fire with coal oil, and then lynched on the normally peaceful town square.

A year after her diary concluded, two black men faced a similar fate. They ambushed and killed a deputy sheriff and wounded the town sheriff, J. B. "Jesse" Butler. After being captured, the two—one already dead and the second severely wounded—were taken by a group of vigilantes a half-mile from the center of the city to Buford Park.[2] Despite the pleas of Butler's wife not to commit this act, the group threw each into a blazing bonfire.

Because of reputation or happenstance, a few years later the high school football team, selected as part of the feature event, played Oak Cliff of Dallas on Ku Klux Klan Day at the State Fair of Texas. The Wednesday afternoon encounter, with three hundred fans and the high school band accompanying the squad to Dallas, saw their undefeated team get white washed 62–0.

With all this swirling about, Alma's naïve clock concerning race and world events was ticking. Like most young whites of the twentieth century, she was caught up in her teen years. Head in the sand? No—just a teenager not caring about a world of uncertainty that was about to erupt into violence at home and abroad. Alma, blinded to anything but her current life, focused on her teenage adventures. Her bias was against any events keeping her from her boyfriend, Emmet.

Alma Weeks Caldwell, born two days before Christmas in December 1896, was from a prestigious bloodline. Her great-grandfather, lawyer, newspaper publisher, and state senator John Almus Gardner was respected enough to have a town named after him in Tennessee.

Her two grandfathers also carried heavy credentials, although favoring different sides during the US Civil War. Credited as a "strong, conservative Union man who worked hard to prevent Tennessee from seceding from the United States," lawyer William Parker Caldwell was, among his many honors, a US House of Representative member from Tennessee for two terms in Washington D.C. with the Forty-Fourth and Forty-Fifth Congresses.

Alma's maternal grandfather, Claiborne Edward Birthright, was an officer in the Missouri State Guard in Dunklin County, Missouri, and fought for the Confederate States of America during the war. After the conflict, Claiborne, better known as "The Colonel" to his many friends, moved his growing family to Texas, where he founded the town of Birthright.

2 A newly acquired seventy-acre city park purchased from Confederate veteran William Buford. The park was located west of the town square and named in Buford's honor.

Dr. Luther Weeks Caldwell

Carrie Birthright

Her father, Dr. Luther Weeks Caldwell was a member of the fifth graduating class at Vanderbilt Medical School in Nashville, Tennessee. In 1880, Dr. Caldwell relocated to Sulphur Bluff, Texas to start his practice. There he met and courted Alma's mother, Carrie Birthright.

The glowing account of their May 1887 nuptials in the local paper stated:

> Dr. Luther Caldwell and Miss Carrie Birthright were united in marriage at the residence of the bride's parents on the evening of the 24th, Rev. P.C. Archer officiating. After the ceremony was performed, the guests, who were numerous, repaired to the residence of Mr. James Mellown where a handsome supper awaited them. When all had been done full justice to this part of the program the sweet strains of the violin were heard and soon the spacious hall was a scene of merriment indescribable.
>
> In the midst of this gayety the moments flew by unheeded until a late hour when all went to their respective homes with hearts full of praise

> for those who had afforded them an evening of so great pleasure and many are the kind wishes for the talented and successful young physician and his truly lovely and intellectual young bride, whose friends are numerous is a synonym for all that is womanly and pure. (*Sulphur Springs Gazette,* May 1887)

Alma grew up in a happy home along with three treasured sisters, Lou Ada, Mattie Ruth, and Grace Byron. The Caldwell's third child and only son, five-year-old William Claiborne, forever remembered to the children as "Little Brother," tragically passed away only one month before Alma was born.

Their lives were enjoyable despite Dr. Caldwell's declining health. His arthritic condition became so restrictive that he gave up his medical practice when he was forty-nine years old. Looking for a new source of income, Caldwell, in 1904, moved his family thirty-five miles west to Commerce, Texas, to open a shoe store, Caldwell and Hardin. When that venture failed in 1911, the family made their last move to 933 Davis Street in Sulphur Springs, Texas.

In February 1888, Caldwell bought the farm area and the structure on Davis Street from his father in law for $1,162.50. It even included a historic well, which was touted as having the sweetest tasting water in town. It was from this home that Alma wrote the yearlong story of her life.

933 Davis St.

Dozier Thornton

Emmet Thornton

Emmet Thornton, born in 1896, also came from a well-respected family tree. His grandfather, Howard Brazelton Putnam—touted by the *Sulphur Springs Gazette* on March 8, 1921 as "a pioneer of Hopkins County citizenship"—was an honored Confederate soldier who fought in the Civil War and reluctantly surrendered with the greatest general of his time, Robert E. Lee, at Appomattox in 1865.

Emmet's father Judge Dozier Thornton dominated the Sulphur Springs political scene for many years. His love of civic work included being a prominent county attorney, president of the school board for nineteen years, president of the Chamber of Commerce, president of the Guaranty State Bank & Trust, and a successful lawyer. Still, at his death in 1921, he was more recognized for what the local paper praised as "generous, kindhearted, and of impeachable character. He was often referred to as a man whose heart was as large as his body" (*Sulphur Springs Gazette*, March 8, 1921).

Emmet was the eldest child of Dozier and wife Maggie Putnam Thornton. The household included two sisters, Laura and Rose, and a brother, Morris.

While Alma was jotting down life day by day in her diary, her home state of Texas, although bigger than many European nations in total land mass, contained less people within its borders in 1913 than the much

FUNERAL NOTICE

The friends and acquaintances of Mrs. Carrie Caldwell are respectfully invited to attend the funeral of her husband,

DR. L. W CALDWELL,

From the family residence on Davis street this afternoon. Services and burial at City Cemetery at 4:00 o'clock.

Sulphur Springs, Texas, Thursday, April 25th, 1912.

Funeral notice

smaller state of Ohio. The population was a little more than four million people with 71 percent being white Americans. San Antonio was the state's largest city, followed closely by a booming Dallas with 100,000 residents. Her hometown of Sulphur Springs had only 5,110 citizens.

The hamlets of various states were filled with breathtaking events in 1912. In April, the RMS *Titanic* was lost on its maiden voyage. Every city paper begged for more headlines of the unsinkable ship's demise and its loss of 1,517 passengers. The United States welcomed New Mexico as state number forty-seven, followed a month later by number forty-eight, Arizona. It would be almost a half-century before another state would join the Union.

Less than two weeks after the sinking of the RMS *Titanic*, Alma's father slipped from her life. Only fifty-six, he passed away on April 24. The city newspaper concluded, "his life was clean, clear, and he was a square man. He was a successful practitioner, good business man and left his financial affairs in excellent condition" (*Sulphur Springs Gazette*, April 25, 1912).

In 1913, Woodrow Wilson became the twenty-eighth President of the United States. Still, the big news was not about a new president, but the accomplishments of an automobile builder named Henry Ford. He established the first assembly line for major production in his plant in Highland Park, Michigan. His Ford Model-T automobiles, first produced in 1908, were pulled along a 250-foot-long assembly line with various workers adding parts as each vehicle passed by. With Ford's automobiles assembled at a record pace, the availability of the Motel-T boomed.

The rest of Alma's life would spiral through the slightly warped twentieth century, featuring her love with Emmet, family, and unfortunate despair. Regardless of the future calendar of events, for a spectacular twelve months it was a young girl giggling over, fighting with, denying, flirting, and eventually falling in love with the one who would become her lifetime partner. And it all started in 1913.

2

Summer of Fun

"Upon answering it, I found it to be Emmet Thornton, a schoolmate, to my surprise, wanting a date with me to go to church which I accepted with pleasure. I enjoyed his company very much that nite."

The summer of fun hovered around local churches, small refreshment shops, the popular telephone, touring in the "Tin Lizzie" Ford Model-T automobile, train rides, and the other blossoming teenage thrill, movie houses. Teenagers could catch any number of vaudeville acts or silent movies ("moving pictures") in Sulphur Springs at the Jefferson, the Lyrics, the Buford, or the Mission theaters.

The sudden explosion of stories filmed in New York and the new movie productions from California stirred many a heart. The black-and-white and sometimes-tinted pictures, onscreen intertitles, extreme actor body language, highlighted by the sounds of local piano players, brought a new thrill to many small towns. Until communication inventions introduced the "viral age" in the early twenty-first century, no time saw a greater change in the standards of daily teenage adventures than Alma's generation did.

Sunday June 15, 1913

Rodger Wilson was visiting here from Terrell. I had a date with him Sunday afternoon to go Kodaking with a bunch of girls. The crowd met at my house including Pauline Ripley, Edith Barker, Ruth McCorkle, Hazel Ripley, and Jim Wester. We went all over town that afternoon.

Ego Birthright

Made 12 good pictures and also went by the Candy Kitchen[1] and got something to drink. Sunday nite I went to church with Ego Birthright (uncle)[2] and we got to church too late, so fifteen of we girls sat on the grass that nite till church was over. The crowd consisted of Tonye Nunn, Marguerite Brown, Vera Gee, Sue Letta Bullock, Annie Bohannon, Hazel Ripley, Mary Gibson, & Mildred Woods. I met Mary Gibson that nite. Think she is awfully cute.

Monday June 16, 1913

Today we went on a picnic to Colonel's Camp,[3] and believe me we had a good time. While coming home it rained on us and we were feeling "delightful". The crowd consisted of Vera Gee, Edith Barker, Tonye Nunn, Ruth Brashear, Laurette Ponder, Pearl Parker, & myself. (Boys) Bascom Bingham, Tom McElvey, Aubrey Westbrook, Mrs. Warren and Mrs. Nunn chaperone.

Tuesday June 17, 1913

About 3:30 P.M. while embroidering, being all alone, unexpectedly the telephone rang. Upon answering it, I found it to be Emmet Thornton, a schoolmate, to my surprise,

1 The American Candy Kitchen, site of homemade candies and ice cream, was one of the best known in the city. Its renowned soda fountain highlighted by the variety of cold drinks and chocolates made it a teenager favorite.

2 Ego was the son of Colonel Claiborne Edward Birthright from his second marriage. Although an uncle, he was a year younger than Alma was. He would serve in World War I and suddenly die in 1919.

3 The Colonel's Camp was a site owned by the late Colonel Birthright at his namesake Birthright, Texas.

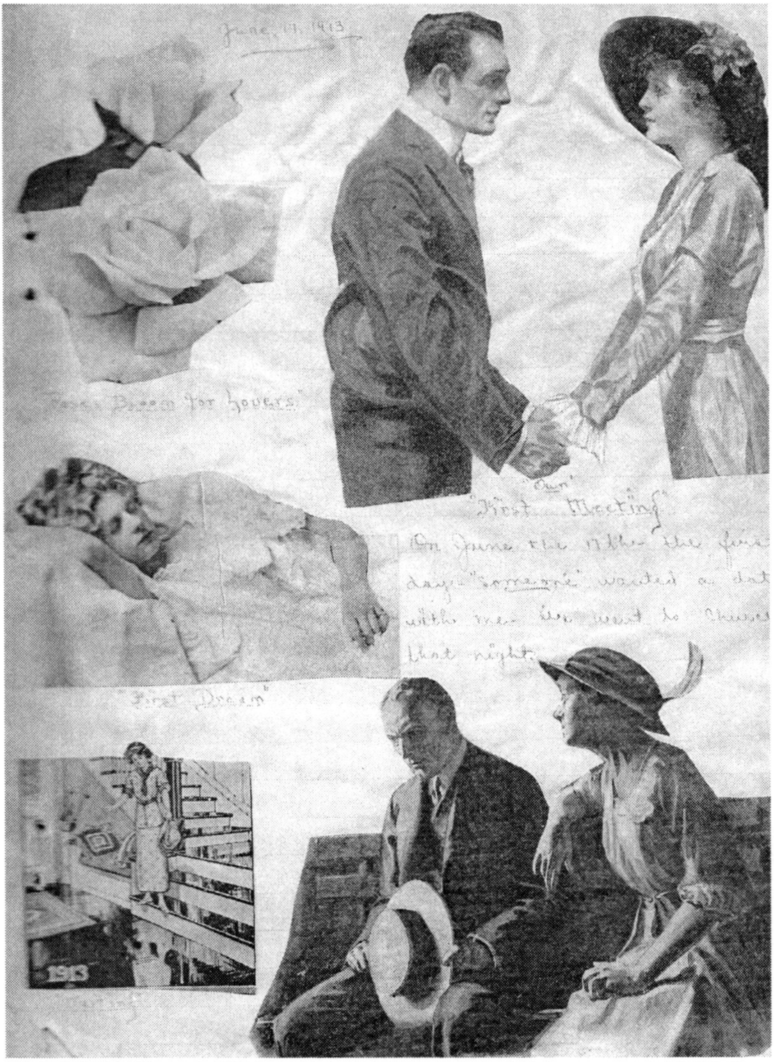

Scrapbook page of first date

wanting a date with me to go to church, which I accepted with pleasure. I enjoyed his company very much that nite.

Wednesday June 18, 1913

I had a date with Emmet, and we went to prayer meeting at the "First Baptist Church." We had an awful good time.

"Sister" Lou Ada Caldwell

Sunday June 22, 1913

I went driving this evening with Jewell Cambron and Edith Barker and stayed at home that nite and read a book through.

Wednesday June 25, 1913

Edith spent the nite with me, and I had a date with Guinea Thomas and Edith Barker had a date with Ben Buford. We intended on going to the show but it rained so we could not. We cracked nuts and ate fruit till we almost killed ourselves.

Sunday June 29, 1913

Miss Mattie McCauley, Sister and myself went to the Methodist Church. We all stopped at Miss Mattie's after church and had some music.

Wednesday July 2, 1913

We all went to the show. There was Vera McCauley, Mattie & Sister & myself. Had the best time.

Sunday July 6, 1913

Emmet and myself started to church but got there too late so we met Tonye & Edith & Tom Lewis. We all started to the Palace of Sweets[4] together but Emmet and myself went to the Bakery- "C"- I bid him good-by at the Bakery. William McDonald wanted a date with me but I had a date so I refused him.

4 The Place of Sweets had been destroyed by fire in May. It was "reinstalled at the same stand, under the same name, and management" in late June (*Sulphur Springs Gazette*, June 20, 1913).

Grace Caldwell

Monday July 7, 1913

I have nearly worked my little self to death today getting my things ready to leave. Uncle Harvey Caldwell is visiting us from Mineral Wells, Texas. He has been teasing me all day about someone.

Tuesday July 8, 1913

I spent all morning in town and went down to see Edith Barker. She was ironing—(so hard). I stayed at home all afternoon.

Wednesday July 9, 1913

About 12:30 the telephone rang (wanted to know if I was going to leave that day I said yes). It was a boy but I don't know who he was but I have an idea. He said he wanted to tell me goodbye. Grace and myself left on evening train[5] and was accompanied by Flora Thomas, Myrtle Knight, and Ruth Patterson of Rosell. We were met in Commerce by Hazel Horton at the station. That afternoon Hazel and I went to the city. After parading around the square, I met all my old boy friends.[6] That night I had a date and we went to the show.

Thursday July 10, 1913

Hazel and I went to town and I met all the girls and talked to the boys. They all seem very glad to see this girl once more.

5 The train station, located north of the town square near Alma's home, was for the St. Louis Southwestern Railway, which was also well known to local East Texans as the "Cotton Belt" Railroad. Passenger trains were a major means of transportation between Sulphur Springs and Commerce because of the uncertainty of the condition of unpaved roads between the two towns.

6 The Caldwell girls attended Commerce schools after their father opened a shoe store in the city in 1904. This trip was returning to see old schoolmates. While in Commerce, they stayed at the home of R. D. Horton and family.

Specially <u>two</u> boys. My old <u>friends</u>. This was the first day of the picnic, in <u>Commerce</u>.[7] While coming from town there were 7 girls in the bunch. We met Soda Reynolds in his touring car. He carried us to Cumby that morning. The girls were Hazel, Willie Gamble, Elizabeth Gamble of Greenville, Pearlle Hickerson, Bernice [Naler], & myself & Soda. That afternoon we went to the ball game (Cumby & Commerce). I went with Neal Barker—Hazel with Baine Pierce. We went to the picnic grounds that <u>nite</u> and had more fun and joy.

Friday July 11, 1913

I sent 15 cards home (to Sulphur Springs). Hazel & I spent the day with Mary & Ollie Prim. We all had dates that evening and we went up to Willie Gambles and danced all afternoon. We then went to town to the <u>Palace of Sweets</u> for something to drink and to the Post Office. I received a card from my (lover) stating he would be in Commerce the next day. We all spent the nite with Mary & Ollie Prim. There were seven girls. We had dates and went to the show. Had just oodles of fun. Yes we did.

Saturday July 12, 1913

We girls went car riding. That afternoon, we met the 4:30 train. There were Mary & Ollie Prim, Neva Noland, & Hazel & myself. <u>Mr. Emmet Thornton</u> and James Wester came from home. We went through town on out home that afternoon. About 6:30 Mr. [Earnest] Prim carried all of us car riding then we let the boys out in town and we went the picnic grounds and had a spread. Believe me we had some fun that nite. There were 10 couples that left the grounds at once about 11 o'clock. We reached home about 12 o'clock (remember the distance). The <u>nite</u> was beautiful. We all sat out on

7 The big Ninth Annual Picnic in Commerce opened a three-day celebration with a decorated car parade, featured visiting speakers debating current issues, fireworks displays every night, a "Farmers' Day," and an "Educational Day," honoring students of East Texas Normal College.

the beautiful lawn until the late hour and at 1:30 we departed. We girls then retired about 2:30.

Sunday July 13, 1913

I was awaken[ed] by the sound of the telephone ringing. It was Emmet. They had decided to remain in Commerce till the next day. We went to Sunday School that morning and went to the station that eve to see the boys leave coming home. Believe me, I did want to come. We had been at Mary's house but a little while when the telephone rang. Hubert Knox wanted a date with me for that afternoon. We all went walking and that nite I had a date with Grover Sellers. We went to church at the Methodist Church and from there to the Palace of Sweets. We all went home and made candy that nite out at Mary and Ollie Prim's home. The boys left late that nite but we had so much fun.

Monday July 14, 1913

I spent the day with Gertrude Mayes. I had a delightful time. We went driving that morning and to the club that afternoon. About 4:30 P.M. the telephone rang for me. To my surprise, it was a call from Sulphur Springs (from him). He wanted to know when I was coming home. Mrs. Earnest Prim gave a party that nite in my honor. I went with Ben Kelly. I enjoyed Ben's company very much that nite and had a grand time at the party.

Wednesday July 16, 1913

I awoke [and] found myself at Gertrude['s]. She had prepared for a big Porch Party at 8 o'clock. We rushed around. I soon found myself seated at the table playing rook with 25 girls on the porch. I bid the girls & boys of Commerce farewell at 1:10 that afternoon. The following were at the station Leah Jaynes, Eugenia Ridley of Rosenberg, Texas, Hazel Horton, Ollie and Mary Prim & Ben Kelly. We made some pictures at the station of which two were good. As the train pulled out, tears came I guess. Don't know. Reached home all O.K. and found Sister to meet us. Her chum had come down on the same train (Miss Maggie Murray). Had not been at home very long till the telephone rang. Discovered it to be Mr. Emmet Thornton wanting a date that nite. We spent the time at home which was enjoyed by both ……"C"

A JOLLY PORCH PARTY

One of the jolliest parties given in Commerce was that of Wednesday morning from 8 to 10 in the honor of Miss Alma Caldwell of Sulphur Springs, and Miss Vera Johnson of Iowa Park, at the home of Miss Gertrude Mayes on Sycamore Street.

The porch was lavishly decorated in ferns and sunflowers which made it a thing of beauty. The register was an unique conception which was presided over by little Miss Ethel Hooser. From there the guests were shown to the punch bowl where Grace Caldwell and Melba Moreland served grape juice.

After the guests had all arrived the rest of the time was spent playing rook which was enjoyed by all. After a delicious ice course the many guests departed hoping that Miss Mayes would entertain the visiting girls again soon.

The guests were Misses Gertrude Mayes, Alma Caldwell, Vera Johnson, Elizabeth Gamble of Greenville, Minnie Lee Todd of Texarkana, Lorraine Parten, Eugenia Ridley of Rosenberg, Pearlle Hickerson, Bernice Naler, Ollie Prim, Lois Holder of Brasher, Mary Prim, Edith Wheeler, Leah Jaynes, Melba Tipton of Ft.

The Kodak moment taken at the Commerce Cotton Belt Depot. Grace Caldwell, Alma Caldwell, Ollie Prim, Leah Jaynes, Vera Johnson, Hazel Horton, and Mary Prim

> Smith, Arkansas, Fay Goodman of Dallas, Ethel Hooser, Grace Caldwell of Sulphur Springs, Mrs. C. S. Mayes, Mary Johnson of Iowa Park, and Melba Moreland. (*The Commerce Journal*, July 18, 1913)

Thursday July 17, 1913

I spent the day sleeping and telling of my "Romantic Trip" to the city of Commerce.

Sunday July 20, 1913

Miss Maud Ramey spent the day with us. It rained all day long. We planned to go Kodaking but our plans fell through. I stayed at home that nite.

Wednesday July 23, 1913

Edith Barker spent the day with me. She had a date with Glynn Pickett that nite. I had a date with Emmet Thornton. We had planned to go to a (watermelon) cutting at the High

School but we did not. It was impossible for me to go to the show that nite. (mother disapproved) "C" so we walked a part away to town with Glynn & Edith. They went to the show. I had a real good time that nite.

Sunday July 27, 1913

Emmet wanted a date I refused & also William McDonald. Ben Kelly came down with Neal Barker & he came out to see me. Edith & Tonye spend the nite with me. Somebody I think is mad. "C"

Wednesday July 30, 1913

We are going to have a spread (Southern picnic). I was getting ready to go when a car stopped. To my surprise found it to be Mary & Ollie Prim from Commerce. We all went to town and bought our dinner. From there we went to Tonye's and Edith and met the crowd. The crowd was comprised of Hazel Ripley, Jewell Cambron, Edith Barker, Tonye Nunn, Marquerite Brown, Annie Bohannon, Sue Letta Bullock, Ollie Prim, Mary Prim, Gladys Keeney and myself. I can't say I enjoyed myself very much that day but I will overlook it as it was somebody's fault and not mine. I hope I will never interfere as I did that day between two parties. The day would have been more pleasanter for both without me. I was to blame I guess. That evening we girls went to town. That nite Ollie had a date with Glynn Pickett, Mary with Jim Wester, and me with E.T. We stayed at home that nite. I learned something that nite I will never forget or will tell unless things change from what they are now. "C"—(Secret)

Thursday July 31, 1913

Mary, Ollie, & myself went to town that morning and ate dinner with Miss Jessie Butler.[8] The girls left that morning. Had an awful good time. Hated to see the girls leave.

---

8 Miss Jessie Butler was the daughter of City Sherriff Jessie Butler and his wife Emma. She was called "Miss Jessie Butler" to avoid confusion.

Scrapbook page of summer picnic

Friday August 1, 1913

Sallie Pate had a party (watermelon). I spent the nite with Edith Barker & Tonye Nunn. Hazel Ripley also spent the night. Edith had a date with Neal Barker from Commerce. Believe me we had <u>oodles</u> of fun that night. Lester Smith came home (to see Edith) with me. He is one more sight.

Saturday Aug 2, 1913

I received a letter from Neal Barker and Ollie Prim from Commerce.

Sunday August 10, 1913

This was a real lonesome day to me for I spent most of the day by myself. Emmet phoned me from Elberta Lake[9] that morning. I had a date that nite we went to church.

Monday August 11, 1913

This was the first day of the old "Settlers Reunion." That afternoon I met the 2:10 train expecting Hazel Horton, Mary Prim and Neva Noland but Mary was the only one that came. Winnie Kenyon also came from Cooper. Mary spent the nite with Miss Jessie Butler that nite. They all went to the show.

BIG CROWDS GATHER AT OLD SETTLERS RE-UNION AT OAK PARK

The program for the first day began at ten o'clock, the White Oak band drawing the crowd with stirring music. Dr. J. P. Dickerson, President of the Re-union Committee, made an excellent opening address, which was followed by a few good talks from other old settlers.

At 2:30 p. m. Uncle Howard Hargrave delivered a lengthy address, his subject being "The History and Development of Hopkins County." In his address he took occasion to pay eloquent tribute to the lives of Tuck Sparks and other deceased settlers. (*Sulphur Springs Gazette*, August 15, 1913)

9 Elberta Lake, classified as a "reservoir" by the state, is a manmade lake located southeast of Sulphur Springs. It had been dug with the use of mules in 1906. The Dozier Thornton cabin was the first lake house built there.

Tuesday Aug 12, 1913

Mother was sick in bed. Had the doctor for the first time that morning with her. Mary and Winnie spent the day with me. We went to town that morning. Met Emmet and we all got something to drink. We all had a date that nite. Mary Prim with Earnest Deakins, Winnie with Glynn Pickett and me with Emmet. We all intended on going to the show but Mother was too sick to leave.

SECOND DAY

At 10:30 a. m. on the second day T.C. McCorkle filled the vacancy in the program occasioned by the absence of Hon. Louis J. Wortham of Fort Worth. Mr. McCorkle made a highly interesting speech which was well received.

In the afternoon Hon. J. H. Davis made a splendid address in the interest of the Southern States Cotton Corporation and 15 cent cotton. This matter is of vital interest to the people and Mr. Davis was given close attention. He is greatly pleased with the progress the Corporation has made and is sure of its ultimate success. (*Sulphur Springs Gazette,* August 15, 1913)

Wednesday August 13, 1913

Mother little better. This was the last day of the Reunion. We had planned to take supper at the Reunion that nite. That afternoon we all went to town. Emmet walked home with us (to Mrs. Butlers). I did not get to go that nite, but the rest did. They had a delightful time. Only one accident. Miss Jessie Butler broke her toe (that was her hard luck). She was an invalid the next 5 days. Could not walk for a week.

LAST DAY

The big three days session of the Old Settlers Re-union at Oak Park closed last night with a tremendous crowd in attendance and another big and successful Re-union has passed into history.

This is the eighth year the Re-union has been held at Oak Park, and Messrs. J. A. Stevenson & Sons have always exerted their best facilities to made the Re-union a success. The last day of the Re-union was given over to Fraternalism and Our United Brotherhood was much in evidence. The O. U. B. Band from Winnsboro was on hand to assist in the music. (*Sulphur Spirngs Gazette*, August 15, 1913)

Thursday August 14, 1913

I went over to Mrs. Butler's after Mary. Winnie had gone to the country but was coming back that afternoon. Bernice Paturn was going to have a dance that night in honor of Miss Hox from Paris. She put me with Jack Sly. He made his date but I could not go because Mother was too sick. Mary and Winnie spent the night with Miss Jessie and they went. They enjoyed their selves very much. I stayed at home that nite with Mother.

Friday August 15, 1913

Winnie went to the country. Mary spent the day with me. Mother was some better this morning. Mary intended on going home that day but changed her mind later. That morning Mary and I went to town and I certainly was treated cool by a certain person. Just barely spoke—maybe not to me. We went to the Palace of Sweets to get something to drink. We met Mr. Crosby from Gilmer. About 2:30,

Thurman Davis phoned and wanted a date with me. Said he would bring Mr. Crosby to see Mary. So we accepted. That nite ever remember Mary played—"Floreine Waltz"[10] one dozen times before they came. Ha! Ha! Ha! They lost the way and went to Mr. Beasley. Believe me somebody had a sore foot and could hardly walk. I will never forget the diamonds we wore that nite.

Saturday August 16, 1913

Mary and I went town that morning. Had more fun. Saw Mr. Crosby. Told him good bye. Mary left that afternoon on the evening train. Believe me this was the hottest day I ever saw. Emmet, Ego and Jimmie came to the station that evening. I saw Miss Kate Lindley on the train. She was on her way to Colorado Springs. She look good to me. Myrtle [Crisp], Sister & myself went to town that evening. Stayed at home that nite.

Sunday August 17, 1913

Mary Pate, Sallie [Pate] & Mamie Rash and I went driving that afternoon. Had more fun. A certain boy wanted a date with me (won't mention his name) but I had a date. We stayed at home that nite.

Wednesday August 20, 1913

Emmet and myself went to Prayer meeting. We went by and got Miss Era Stevenson and her friend from Dallas. Ever remember that night.

Thursday August 21, 1913

Edith phone[d] me this morning that she was going to spend the day with me so she came over to the house about 8 o'clock

10 The "Floreine Waltz" was one of the earliest pieces in the popular series of syncopated waltzes.

Edith Barker

that morning. We did nothing that day but embroidery on a garment for Edith. That afternoon the telephone rang. It was Emmet wanting to know if I wanted to go to the party that nite at Mrs. [John] Westbrook in honor of her sister in law of Ft. Worth Miss B. B. Westbrook. I said well we will go, but gee I wish we hadn't gone. That nite as I was waiting for Emmet to come someone whistled. I went to the door and it was Bascom Bingham, Edith Barker & Tonye Nunn. They brought E.T. out to the house in the buggy. I got in the buggy and they carried us to the party. O! but that was one more nite. I shall never, never forget it. No never. That nite I thought the distance increased a mile a minute. I can account for it (though) "C"

Sunday August 24, 1913

I had a date with Emmet. Things were not very pleasant for either of us. "C" (I wonder why) (Nobody knows but us)

Monday August 25, 1913

I went to Birthright. Had the best time. We went car riding and horseback riding & did everything for amusement. I wrote 5 letters while out there. Two to S.S. & two to Commerce & one to Memphis, Texas.

Monday September 1, 1913

I came home early this morning from Birthright in a car.[11] I went to town this afternoon and Emmet Thornton walked part of the way home with me. I didn't know whether anyone was glad to see me return or not. I guess not.

Wednesday September 3, 1913

We went to Prayer Meeting but got there too late so went to the show. Had oodles of fun.

Sunday September 14, 1913

I had a date with Emmet. Some boy phoned and wanted a date whose name I don't know. We stayed at home that next morning being school morning. "C"

11 Automobiles were so new, rules were being created as need arose. One major problem in Sulphur Springs was the drivers not obeying a new law concerning cars driven in the city. The *Gazette* reported on September 5 "Monday morning there were nine automobiles arraigned in the city corporation court, charged with driving without tail lights. There was no other charge against the accused, such as exceeding the speed limit, and as this was the first time that this law has been enforced here, Judge Field let them off without a fine, but warning them never to do it again, that no excuse whatever of failure to have a tail light would be considered; that the ordinance would be rigidly enforced from now on."

3
School Days

"Ever remember today. I am seventeen. I feel quite old for some reason."

Sulphur Springs High School

Sulphur Springs High School was a short walking distance south of the Caldwell home. The school year of 1913–1914 found Alma in the tenth grade and Emmet starting his senior year. In the Texas education system, students received their high school diplomas after successfully completing the eleventh grade. High school started at 9 AM, closed at noon and reopened at 1 PM with school ending at 4 PM. Pupils were not permitted to enter the building or grounds more than thirty minutes before the opening hour nor were they allowed to loiter on the premises after school.

Education, along with the church activities, dominated the time of most teenagers in the city. This rural community was proud of the fact "the school now has enough units of affiliation with the University of Texas and the other leading Universities and Colleges of Texas. Our graduates can now enter any of these schools without examination" (from the *Course of Study Rules and Regulations for the Public Schools of Sulphur Springs Independent School District*).

Alma and Emmet's course of study for their two grade levels included classes chosen from the following subjects:

Tenth Grade
English: American Literature. Study Three of College Entrance Requirements. Home reading.
Mathematics: Wentworth and Smith's Plane Geometry, Books I, II, III, IV.
History: Andrew's English History.
Latin: One book of Caesar and four orations of Cicero. Latin grammar and Prose composition.
Chemistry: Brownlee and others.
Manual Training:[1]
Domestic Economy: Household Chemistry.
Sewing:
Agriculture:

Eleventh Grade
English: English Literature and Classics completed. Review English Grammar, Theme Writing.
Mathematics: Plane and Solid Geometry.
History: First Term, Cousin and Hill's American History.
Second Term, James and Sanford Civics.
Physics: Cahart and Chute.
Latin: Cicero's Manilian Law. Vergil's Aeneid, three books. Latin Grammar and prose composition.
Manual Training:

1 Manual Training was installed for the boys as their vocational work. The word *manual* meant making things by hand. The course was subdivided into "Mechanical Drawing" and "Bench Work." Mechanical drawing was the planning or designing of things that a student might have a talent he could develop. Bench Work was the practical side of Manual Training. It was in this section that the boys had benches with saws, hammers, and such so they could develop materials into some definite form as directed by their instructor, E. A. Haynie. Haynie was also the high school principal.

Domestic Economy: Advanced Cooking, Sewing.
Agriculture: Agricultural Chemistry.

Monday September 15, 1913

(Received my first note from E.). School started this morning. The vacation is over. Most of the fun has ceased.

Sunday September 21, 1913

Went to church and Sunday School Sunday morning. Sunday afternoon Mildred Woods carried me driving.

Sunday October 5, 1913

I remained at home all day and stayed home that nite also Ego came over to the house. Had more fun. Made candy and had good luck.

Friday October 17, 1913

Our "Foot-Ball Team" went to Commerce today. I am sitting here tonight so mad I can hardly write this. I was crazy to go but had a cold. O! this cold. I cried but it didn't do any good this time. I hope our boys will win.

COMMERCE LOSES TO SULPHUR SPRINGS

In one of the hardest fought football games ever played in this section the Sulphur Springs High School team defeated the local school team by a score of 6 to 0 last Friday. There really should have been no scoring but the officials [referee Miller of East Texas Normal College and umpire Rutland of Cornell] got their downs mixed up giving the visitors a fifth down in which to make ten yards, they making their lone touchdown on this.

Glynn Pickett

It was fourth down with 8 yards to go. [Drue] Connally tried to make this around right end: he failed to gain. Here the ball should have gone over, but Sulphur was allowed another trial through the fact that the referee was misinformed in regard to the down. On the fifth down [Glynn] Pickett got by the left end for a touchdown. Commerce was on Sulphur's three yard line twice and lost the ball through the officials inability to keep up with the downs. A good crowd of citizens and students attended the first game and it is to be hoped that they will continue to give their support to a team that so highly deserves it. (*Commerce Journal*, October 24, 1913)

Sunday October 19, 1913

I had a date. We stayed home & talked about Commerce. About the game.[2]

Friday October 24, 1913

The Speer College football boys came and played S. S. boys. Sulphur won 25-0. I went to the game with Maggie

---

2 Sulphur Springs High School had previously played only a two games in school history. A contest in 1911 with King's Seminary resulted in a Sulphur Springs' 6–0 win. The school's *Tattler* publication noted from that game "All of the High School boys came out with scratches or minus a shirt." There was a single game in 1912, producing a 9–0 win over Commerce. Principal Haynie, because the game was not confined to just students, booted a thirty-yard drop kick in it. With his extra down dash, Pickett's score was the first individually reported touchdown in what would become an illustrious Sulphur Springs' football history.

Sherwood and Nona Williams.[3] I will ever remember that afternoon.

Saturday October 25, 1913

Ruth McCorkle spent the day with me. We had more fun. She also spent the nite with me. We were crazy to go to the show but had no one to go with us.

Friday October 31, 1913

Mrs. Levi Bird gave a Halloween party. I was dressed as little Red Riding—(red). Went with Emmet Thornton. He was not masked. Had a very good time, cutting up with everybody.

Sunday November 2, 1913

I was so cold all day. I stayed at home and read all day. I had a date but didn't accept. (too cold) "C"

Friday November 7, 1913

Had more fun in school. The Foot-Ball boys went to Mt. Pleasant that afternoon.[4] Mary Carter came from Winnsboro that day. Maggie Sherwood is going to give her a party tonite. My name was sent to Hart Longino. He sent Maggie a letter stating that he was sorry but had had a date for a week for that nite. Kathleen Yantis spent the nite with me. She had a date with Maurice Ferguson. I went with them. Had a very good time.

Saturday November 8, 1913

Miss Hazel Ripley gave a slumber party in honor of Miss Mary Gibson. I had a date with Emmet T. She also had a

3 The cost to see a Sulphur Springs game at the "Football Park" near the Cotton Belt track was fifteen cents for students and twenty-five cents for the general public.

4 The team went to Mt. Pleasant to play the Speer's College team. The Speer School for Boys was in existence from 1912 to the spring of 1914 before closing as a result of lack of attendance. The *Gazette* reported the game as the local team "came back a sadder and wiser bunch of boys—the score being 59–6 in favor of Mt. Pleasant. However they have plenty of 'explanations' as to how it happened" (November 14, 1913).

Theater Party that nite. I can't say I had a very good time that nite after the boys came. Things seem to be in confusion in some way.

Present—

Girls	Boys
Mary Gibson	Roy Lundy
Pauline Ripley	Lester Smith
Alma Caldwell	Emmet Thornton
Jewel Cambron	Robert Mack
Maggie Sherwood	Carter Minter
Edith Barker	Glynn Pickett
Hazel Ripley	Ernest Deakins

More about that nite. I kinder feel that I was in the way. Yet (between two people) for what I have heard I hope I was not. I will ever remember this nite for several reasons. Some I cannot put here in pencil but hope to remember as long as I can. I can't say I had a very good time after the boys came. That nite Mrs. [Charlie] Ripley had the beds numbered 1, 2, and 3. Luck will have it, Edith & I got to sleep together in the choice room—Hazel's nice bed room. Had bad dreams. "C"

Sunday November 9, 1913

We girls awoke very early finding ourselves at Miss [Hazel Ripley's] home on Depot Street. Enjoyed a delightful breakfast and started getting ready for Sunday School. We all went to the Baptist Sunday School. From there we went to the Palace of Sweets, went back to church, and Jewell Cambron spent the day with me. I came through town and got some Kodak films. We intended of going Kodaking that afternoon. Pauline Ripley and Edith Barker came out to my house that afternoon. We started out. Went to town and gee! We were treated cool by everybody we met—especially me by somebody. I didn't care though. Maybe somebody thought

Scrapbook page of the Ripley party

I did. We changed our minds about going Kodaking and went to the B.Y.P.U.[5] at the Baptist Church. I never spent such a miserable afternoon in my life. I hope I will never again. I went home that eve and stayed at home that nite. Like to have died with the blues. Wouldn't anyone try to console whatever.

5 The letters stood for Baptist Young Peoples Union.

It seems that everybody had something against me. Mildred Woods and Tonye brought me home in the buggy.

Monday November 10, 1913
(This week will be omitted) No importance happened. It seems like a century to me for some reasons. Don't know.

Sunday November 16, 1913
I went to Sunday school that morning. Ruth McCorkle and I stayed for church at the Methodist Church. I spent the day with Ruth. Enjoyed the day very much. To my surprise (I was really shocked) I was called to the telephone about 3:50 o'clock. You may guess who it was? I didn't think I would ever have the pleasure in accepting another date with that person from what I had heard the past week he had said about me. Perhaps things had been proved untrue what he had heard—I hope so. I accepted the date. That afternoon after I reached home Edith Barker and I went car riding—had more joy. That nite after we got home from church we both approached the subject of the recurrence of the past week which I will never forget. We took time to sum up a few little incidents that had happened the past 6 months we had gone together. A few things were straight[ened] up yet a few were not. Maybe someday they will be explained more clearly then I could have explained them. Better proof then I could have given. I hope so.

Monday November 17, 1913
This week was more pleasant for me and everyone else for I think the past week seemed to enthuse more than two.

Sunday November 23, 1913
I spent the day very lonesome. Stayed at home all day. I had a date that nite with Emmet.

Monday November 24, 1913

I stayed at home all the rest of this week. This being Thanksgiving we had 3 holidays. Enjoyed them staying at home with Mother.

Friday November 28, 1913

Mother was out at Birthright (city). Myrtle was visiting us. I had a date with Emmet intended of going to the show but Sister interfered.[6] We were entertained part of the time by Myrtle Crisp.

Sunday November 30, 1913

We girls had more fun keeping house. Emmet phone[d] and wanted a date but Sister would not let him come. So that settled the matter. I was shoo nough mad that nite too.

Sunday December 7, 1913

I stayed home all day. Ruth phoned me this afternoon and talked to me a long time. Emmet also phoned me & made a date. We stayed at home, it being too cold to go to church. We used Roy's room[7] that nite. "C"

Monday December 8, 1913

Pauline Ripley's father died at 9:30 P.M. Was buried December 9, 1913. The funeral services were held in the Baptist Church. Edith Barker, Jewell Cambron and myself ordered flowers (carnations) from Greenville. I will never forget that afternoon—no never.

---

6 Sister Lou Ada was eight years older than Alma and in charge when their mother was away.

7 Roy Caldwell and Faugh Pickett rented rooms at the Caldwell home while high school was in session. Roy's father, James P. Caldwell, was a farmer. Faugh's father, Henry W. Pickett, was a doctor in Hopkins County who owned a large farm. The farms were far enough outside the city to require the boys to rent a room during the school year to go to Sulphur Springs High School.

DEATH OF PAUL RIPLEY

Paul Ripley passed quietly to that land of everlasting rest Monday night at 9:30 o'clock, at the home of Mr. and Mrs. J. B. Hinnant, in this city after a long siege of suffering from lung trouble. He was conscious up to the moment of death and was fully prepared, resigned and cheerful, having made every preparation for his funeral. One of his last requests was that his old pastor, Rev. W. B. Vining of Mexia be sent for to conduct the funeral service.

The funeral services were conducted at the Baptist church Tuesday evening at 3:00 o'clock by Rev. Vining. The service was simple, yet of that pathetic heart interest which stirs the soul. Six persons were lead to Christ over his bier, and had it been possible for Paul to have realized this, his spirit would have gone home to God on swifter wings and his harp of gold would have struck even sweeter strains as he entered the choir of Angels. This knowledge will doubtless be imparted to him in the Unknown Land of Peace, and it must bring great joy to his heart to realize that the influence of his pure, Christian life and the example of his noble fortitude lives on, and serves as a beacon of light to lead the hearts of others to Christ.

The interment occurred at the City Cemetery at 4 o'clock and a large concourse of sorrowing relatives and friends were present. The Gazette extends its most sincere sympathies to the bereaved in their great sorrow. *(Sulphur Springs Gazette,* December 12, 1913)

Thursday December 11, 1913

I happened to [have] a very severe accident in the chemical lavatory—cut my arm.

Friday December 12, 1913

Emmet and I are going to the Elks Hall tonite to the "Lyceum Course"[8] Unfortunately they did not come. We went to the show. Emmet gave me some of the prettiest pictures. Had a good time.

Sunday December 14, 1913

I stayed at home all day. Had a date that nite with Emmet but mother thought it best for him not to come so I stayed at home & we had company from Commerce.

Friday December 19, 1913

I had a date with Emmet. We went to the show. Had a good time. As we were coming home that nite we met a woman that had lost her husband. "C" We carried her home. Too bad.

Saturday December 20, 1913

Mother mentioned something to me that I never expect to forget.[9] Something that almost shocked me to death. I hope I never mention this but to one person, which I will the first time I have a chance. I have worried over it all day. I never had anything to worry me anymore in my life. I hope I will never again. Tonite I am sitting here thinking about it. Nobody

8 Lyceums, sponsoring public programs and entertainment, flourished from the mid-nineteenth century into the early twentieth century. In 1915, their numbers totaled at least twelve thousand. Their performances of popular music, dramatic acts, lectures, debates, and vaudeville were held in the small towns of the United States, such as Sulphur Springs, on a single-night basis. They were especially active in northeast Texas during the winter months.

9 Alma's mother revealed to her the shocking revelation her father had committed suicide. It was a tragic family secret, which was very guarded and never discussed. Dr. Caldwell, in terrible pain from his arthritic condition, had chosen to end it. On his tombstone, the truth of his story is in his epitaph: "The pains of health are past. Labor and sorrow cease and life's long warfare closed at last."

knows. Yes, somebody knows for I cannot help but show it. I wish I could see somebody now.

Sunday December 21, 1913

This is Xmas week. Myrtle Crisp marries tomorrow (Monday). Mary Ruth (Mrs. Whittle) came last nite from Caldwell, Kansas to attend the wedding. I went to Sunday School & Church. Edith, Tonye, & Ruth McCorkle spent the day with me. We met the 1:55 train & met Lou Ellene & her husband from Dallas. We also met the 3:15 train to see Hazel leave. She left on the train for Ft. Worth. She gave me a pretty little gift at the station. We all came home, Emmet & the girls & myself and we had not been at home long till the telephone rang. It was some boys wanting dates with the girls. I never felt so bad in my life as I did that eve. I wonder why. The girls stayed till 5:00 and I walked a little piece home with them—"C"—I had a date last nite with Emmet—which this date will always be remembered by me—perhaps nobody else but I hope so. I will not mention anything here, but I will always remember every word which was said between us. I found out what I had been worrying over that was all I cared for "C"

Monday December 22, 1913

Bernice phoned me early this morning and wanted to know if I was going to Myrtle's wedding. It rained all last night and knocked us out of attending the wedding. Emmet & I & Bernice & Malcolm Boyd had planned to go. I received a letter from Ft. Worth today, from Lester [Smith]. Emmet phoned me this morning and wanted to know if we were going to Birthright. I had a long dream last nite (a grand one) about someone. To-morrow is a little girl's birthday. I will be seventeen years old. Vera Gee marries tonite. (to Aubrey Westbrook) I am not going. I sent them the prettiest towel—embroidered by me. I am fixing to write a letter. I wrote 3 this afternoon. I hope I will live till morning for I am crazy for tomorrow to come. "C"

Tuesday December 23, 1913

Ever remember today. I am seventeen. I feel quiet old for some reason. I cooked my first (pie) all by myself without anyone's assistance—a good one too.

Wednesday December 24, 1913

Last nite Dr. Patterson, Mr. & Mrs. [Harry] O'Neil of Dallas, Sister & Emmet & myself went to the show. We had an awful good time. Today it has rained all day long. I went to town this morning. We are going to the Xmas-tree tonite, but it rained so we did not go so we stayed at home. Now we read this diary up to the present date (E & myself). There were many things in the past brought back to our minds. "C" Just as E. was leaving he handed me a tiny box. Upon opening it I found it to be a lovely cameo ring. Something I really wanted. He gave me a great big box of candy for a birthday present (23rd). We enjoyed eating candy after we got through reading this mess. I sent Emmet his laundry bag today. He seemed to be proud of it. (I wonder if he was). Mother gave me a lovely Cameo Lavalier. Roy C gave me a German Silver Vanity Purse. Myrtle Crisp & her husband left today for Clinton Oklahoma to live.

Thursday December 25, 1913

I have spent this Xmas day at home. Glynn and Emmet have gone hunting. I hope they will have good luck & not get hurt. Ego has stayed with us all eve. I have talked to him about a whole lot of little things. He brought me a lovely box of stationary. I certainly was proud of it. I received Miss Lucas (sewing teacher) from Sherman. McGee Long ate dinner with Faugh today. I am going to stay at home tonite & sleep.

Scrapbook page of Our First Christmas

We have planned to go to a big Xmas party tomorrow nite at Marguerite Brown['s]. I wonder where I will be this time next year. I hope I am here though.

Friday Dec 26, 1913

I spent the day at home. About 1:10 o'clock I was called to the telephone. It was Emmet wanting to know if I wanted to go to the party at Marguerite Brown['s] & Sally Pate['s]. We

Scrapbook page of Brown party

first went to the show then from there to the party. Everyone in town was there and all looked pretty. I wore my white dress trimmed with fur. I had a whole lot of fun. Emmet had on a hat. The first one I ever saw him wear. But I did like it on him.

Sunday December 28, 1913

I didn't go to Sunday School or church that day. I was so sick all day I could hardly hold up my head. I wrote a letter to Hazel Ripley in Ft. Worth. Sunday nite I had a date with Emmet. He also wasn't feeling very good that nite so we stayed at home and didn't go to church. So both of us feeling bad. We didn't know of anything to do but quarrel a little, but it didn't amount to anything with either one of us. "C"

Monday December 29, 1913

I have spent the day embroidering. All day long, did not go to the "Social."

Tuesday December 30, 1913

I went to town this morning with Sister. Tonite I have a date with Emmet. He went hunting this morning. Phoned me about 8 o'clock but I didn't know what might happen before nite (somebody might get killed) so I told him to ring me later which he did. So we are not going to fuss tonite but be good. "C"

Wednesday December 31, 1913

I stayed home all day. Guinea Thomas made a date to go to the New Year's dance at the Elks Hall but I did not accept. Also Rayphield Brinker wanted a date with me. Gee! But I am some popular—"C"—I wonder what someone would have thought if I had accepted. Glynn Pickett got hurt today, got shot by accident. I have not heard the particulars yet. Hope he is not hurt very bad. Faugh has gone home. Got a letter from Ollie Prim today.

4
Chilling Winds of Winter

"Oh but I want to go to the Lyceum Course tonite but mother forbids it is too cold. Emmet rang me about 4:30 but I could not go. My, but maybe you think I am not mad. I can hardly write. I really wanted to go tonite."

The year 1914 was another banner one in the establishment of the United States as a major power. In the first half of the year, Americans oversaw the finish of the world's most impressive engineering feat and flexed their military muscles in a conflict with a southern neighbor.

In January, the Panama Canal was the buzz of the country. Completed two years earlier than expected, the fifty-one-mile canal joined the Atlantic Ocean to the Pacific Ocean. In the past, any ship traveling from ocean to ocean had to steer around the southern tip of South America, but the new passage cut across Panama reduced the distance by 7,872 miles.

April exhibited the power of the US military, helping prepare it for the ultimate test three years later. Mexico was in the midst of a ten-year civil war, which deeply concerned Americans.

In the one major military event of Alma's diary time, the United States invaded a port city in neighboring Mexico. On April 21st, US military forces captured Veracruz, Mexico. As a result of poor communication between the governments—the threat of the Germans supplying weapons to Mexican dictator, Victoriano Huerta, and a minor event called the Tampico Affair—President Woodrow Wilson ordered the seizing of the seaport city. After minor casualties to the US army, the invasion force quickly took Veracruz and remained there for the next six months. Huerta would soon lose power and flee in July 1914.

At home in Sulphur Springs, residents struggled with the cold winter weather and the sadness of death. Activities were limited because of the absence of heated transportation, and the untimely death of several in the city, including three going well before their time, made the atmosphere even more frigid. Still, life moved on as did the romance of Emmet and Alma.

Thursday News Year January 1, 1914
I got up this morning feeling kinder tough, but about 3:30 this evening the telephone rang and who should it but "That Old Girl of Mine" Ruth McCorkle (Toosy). We spent this one evening turning over new resolutions for the new year. Gee, but I would hate to repeat some of them. I had a big dish of popcorn—popped when she came popping in. Now, maybe you think we did not devour this. It was delicious. Ruth performed on the piano for me. We merely brought back a few little incidents of our young lives to our minds in words to one another. We will never forget this one afternoon this New Year 1914. I begged Ruth to stay all nite with me but she wouldn't. I am going to the show tonite. Good nite "All Nite Long."

Friday January 2, 1914
I spent the whole day at home. About 3:50 that evening the telephone rang. It was Emmet. Sorry, but I could not accept his date for 3 reasons, which I will not state here. But I did not accept a date, so remained at home all nite. Slept good and had more good dreams about somebody.

Saturday January 3, 1914
I was sick all morning but began feeling better that afternoon so I dressed and went to town and got with Edith & Tonye and

Alma and Beatrice Thornton

Beatrice Thornton. We paraded around town and they walked a piece to Ruth McCorkle's with me. I spent the evening with Ruth. Then Ruth and myself went back to town but I did not see anyone I wanted too. That nite after supper I called up Ego at the Bakery & also Emmet and invited them out to eat dinner with me the next day (Sunday). I talked to E a long time, but honest I didn't call him up.

Sunday January 4, 1914

It is raining hard this morning. Too bad to go to Sunday School so I have dressed waited for the boys to come. Hazel Ripley phoned me and she couldn't eat with me which was too bad. The boys came and we had the best time. The crowd consisted of Emmet Thornton, Ego Birthright, Malcolm Boyd, McGee Long, Roy Caldwell, Faugh Pickett & me. Emmet left about 5:30. I had a date with him that nite. We went to the Methodist Church & mother (the whole family) went also. Now I kinder think we were kinder good tonite. In front of us sat Mother and on the side of us sat Emmet's father. Now, maybe you think we did not act nice. I could tell you ever[y] word the preacher said I believe. Certainly was cold coming home. I like to have frozen.

Monday January 5, 1914

School started this morning beginning another new term.[1] Gee but I heard something today I had not heard before. But, I don't care—no—I don't. It wouldn't do me any good if I did. I got two notes from Emmet today. Oh but I want to go to the Lyceum Course tonite but mother forbids it is too cold. Emmet rang me about 4:30 but I could not go. My, but maybe you think I am not mad. I can hardly write. I really wanted to go tonite. Maybe it is not my fault. I wonder if someone is at the Lyceum Course now and wonder who with—"C". Well I am so sleepy. I will stop this writing. I wonder if someone really wanted me to go to the Lyceum Course. Well, I am sitting up here all by myself. Everyone else is asleep so I will say good nite. Will go to sleep to dream—dream.

Tuesday January 6, 1914

I went to school early this morning & the High School boys & girls went to see the agriculture train that went thru. Believe

1 *The Course of Study Rules and Regulations for the Public Schools of the Sulphur Springs Independent School District* required the janitors for each school to "build fires early in the cold weather and have the room at the proper temperature at the time of opening of school. In the buildings heated by steam or hot air, the janitors shall not be absent from their respective buildings when the heating apparatus is in use."

me I had more fun. There was Hazel, Edith, Pauline, Jewell & myself & Tonye. Tonye found her a friend & we had more fun out of him. He certainly is good looking too. His name was Mr. Coal. Lived in St. Louis, Mo. I got a note from E in school telling me about the Lyceum Course last nite.

Thursday January 8, 1914

Today is the prettiest day. I received 4 notes in school from E.T. Won't mention what was in them.

Friday January 9, 1914

I had a date with E.T. We went to see Marie & Lester Smith had music & had more fun. We intended of going to the show but decided not to go.

Sunday January 11, 1914

E.T. wanted a date but Mother wouldn't let him come. We all (family) went to the Methodist Church. I received a letter from Mary. Answer it today.

Thursday January 15, 1914

Went to school. Left school to attend funeral of Miss Artie Mellown. Came from cemetery with a hot fever. Went to bed and mother was scared and wanted to have a doctor. Was sick all nite.

Friday January 16, 1914

This morning got up feeling better and went to school. They turned school out on account of Mayor Denton being dead. The Rose Maid[2] is going to be played here tonite. E and myself are going. I have been feeling so bad this evening.

---

2 The *Rose Maid*, performed at the Globe Theater in New York from April to September 1912, was an operetta in two acts set in England. Because of its notoriety, the play was performed by vaudeville groups all over the nation in the following years.

Hope I will be feeling better tonite. We went to see Rose Maid. Was real good. Emmet and I both decided to care not what other girls said but to ignore some such as _______.

DEATH OF MAYOR DENTON

Mayor K. T. Denton died on the night of January 15th, without ever having rallied from the stroke of apoplexy with which he was stricken on Tuesday previous.

The funeral services were held at the Baptist church Friday evening at 2:00 o'clock, Revs. Wallace Bassett and J. B. Gober, conducting appropriated and deeply impressive services. The entire city was closed for the funeral and the church was filled to capacity during the services. The remains were laid to rest in the city cemetery at 4 o'clock under the auspices of the Elks Lodge.

The passing of Mayor Denton was a great shock to our people and its suddenness but added to our grief. He was a strong, stalwart, healthy man, apparently in the prime of vigorous manhood, and his demise again emphasizes the fact that we walk in the midst of death and never know the day nor the hour when we will be called from the walks of life.

Mayor Denton's wife died some seven weeks ago, and his grief was pitable: he was a changed man from then on, and confessed religion over the bier of his departed friend, Paul Ripley, a short time thereafter. Those who were intimately associated with Mayor Denton, feel assured that his life and his heart were right with God when the end came, and that

> his spirit has been wafted home to join that of his beloved wife, in the realms of everlasting peace. (*Sulphur Springs Gazette*, January 23, 1914)[3]

Saturday January 17, 1914

Today is Saturday. Keener Minter died yesterday. Age 21. They are going to bury him at Pine Forest tomorrow eve. I am going over there this evening if it doesn't turn colder. I cooked dinner all by myself today. Believe me it was good too. "C"

> **DEATH OF KEENER MINTER**
>
> Keener Minter, son of Mrs. R. A. Minter, died at the family home on College Street in this city, last Friday night, after three weeks suffering. The burial occurred at Pine Forest Cemetery Sunday evening.
>
> The seemingly untimely passing of this excellent young man was a hard blow to his relatives and friends, but we are taught and must believe that the Maker and Shaper of all human destiny, "doeth all things wisely," and that the faithful must ever bear their burdens of grief and sorrow with the hope of a brighter world beyond.
>
> The Gazette extends its kindest sympathies to the bereaved in their great sorrow. (*Sulphur Springs Gazette*, January 23, 1914)

Sunday January 18, 1914

I went to Sunday School this morning & church at the Baptist Church and walked home with Helen [Quinn] and Rebecca

3 Denton was born in 1856. His wife Lizzie, born in 1859, had passed away on November 28, 1913.

[Stribling]. I had a date with E.T. and we went to church but was too late so came home and spent the time. Very pleasant. "C" Get me "Slide". Ida Mae Nelson spent the afternoon with me and we had a bushel of fun.

Monday January 19, 1914

This began a nice week which was not very remarkable with me for I have not written a note this day to E. & honest I have not received one. Now maybe you think I do not feel lost for some cause.

ALMA'S SCHOOL NOTE TO EMMET[4]

Thought you were coming to school this morning. What is the matter not sick I know for I asked Glynn[5] and he said you were combing your hair (he thought) to come to school when he left.

I started to telephone you this morning, but the office was locked and Mr. J— and Mr. H— both had classes so I couldn't get to the telephone. "C" ? But never mind that isn't the only telephone in town and I have a key that gets to a good quiet place hadn't I.

I saw your mother and Mrs. McCauley at noon going I suppose to the cemetery. They was all wrapped up like it was cold but it wasn't.

Here it is 2:30 and I haven't written a note all day (except this little one). School seems so funny. No one to write to. No one to kinder cut my eye at once and a while. Yes it seems mighty strange. This is the first study period that I have been

4 This is the only note exchanged between Alma and Emmet, in the 1913–1914 school year to survive the test of time. There is no date on the letter, but it is an example of what they exchanged at school each day.

5 Faugh Pickett's brother Glynn lived with his senior classmate Emmet during the school year. The Thornton family lived at 318 Church Street, in a home almost directly across from the Methodist Church that their dad bought in 1909. When the home burned many decades later, the Sulphur Springs *Daily News-Telegram* reported "the house was a landmark in Sulphur Springs and at one time was considered a mansion. It was an early-day showplace" (August 15, 1962).

Thornton home

in the study hall to-day. Nobody up here I cared about. What made me want to stay in here? You are coming to school in the morning aren't you? Just for my sake. Good Bye.

Friday January 23, 1914

I received a note from E. Wanted a date but I refused. "C"

Saturday January 24, 1914

Got up real early this morning. Stayed up town till 1:30 o'clock and helped with the Methodist dinner. Surely did have some fun too. The remains of Mrs. Cargile was brought in on the 1:55 train & I met it. Mary Prim from Commerce came. What do you know on that now. We went to the funeral & from there to town. Saw Glynn at the Bakery & Somebody Else. Let me think. Who? "C" We were treated with candy & drinks. Now maybe you think we did not have fun. Came home & E. had phoned wanted a date & bring Ben Buford to see Mary. So they came. We went to the show & to the Palace of Sweets and had more fun. Believe me, I will never forget tonite. No Never for I think something was the matter with somebody. I wonder what? I don't guess I will ever know. No Never "C" O! It seems like old times to have Mary with me.

DEATH OF MRS. B. R. CARGILE

We were sorry to hear of the death of Mrs. B. R. Cargile which occurred in Dallas. Mrs. Cargile lived here for many years and had a host of relatives and friends. (*Sulphur Springs Gazette*, January 30, 1914)[6]

Sunday January 25, 1914

Mary & I went to Sunday school at the Methodist Church. First went to the post office met the girls & Jimmy Wester walked around town with us. From Sunday School we went to church at the Baptist & Emmet came in and sat with us during church. After church we came home and had more fun cutting up. Mary and I went to the train station and there was a big bunch of girls & boys down there. We all wrote Ollie a letter. "C" I came home from the station & spent the rest of the evening with Mrs. Hubbard. Tonite I had company (Ego). We had more fun. We intended of going to church but decided it was much too cold to go so we stayed at home.

6 Alice Cargile, born in 1857, was married to a successful farmer and cattleman in Hopkins County named B. R. Cargile. He lived from 1851 to 1908. They were longtime friends of the Caldwell family.

Monday January 26, 1914

We had our first exam this morning. I think I passed. Received a note from E. this morning in school. "C"

Thursday January 29, 1914

I spent the day with Ida Lindley (Mrs. Chaffin). The remains of her husband was brought in from Oklahoma City last night. He was shot by a negro. It was so sad.

Friday January 30, 1914

I spent the day with Ida.[7] Loraine Parten and Verde Beagen who came down from Commerce to attend the funeral of Mr. Chaffin. E wanted a date that evening but I refused. I had been up so much. Had lost so much sleep.

REMAINS BROUGHT HERE FOR INTERMENT IN CITY CEMETERY

R. L. Lindley and family and Mrs. W.A. Chaffin arrived here Wednesday night, with the remains of Mr. Chaffin and the funeral services will be held at the Lindley home on California street this afternoon at three o'clock Rev. Cephas Shelburne, of Dallas, conducting the services.

The burial occurred at the city cemetery. This is indeed a sad and shocking tragedy and we extend our deepest condolence to the stricken wife and family in their great sorrow.

Oklahoma City, Oklahoma, Jan 26—As the result of one of the boldest holdups and the most cold-blooded shootings that has ever occurred in this city, W. A. Chaffin lies dead at his home, 1600 East 10th Street.

7 Ida would work past the tragedy and remarry in June 1916 to Taylor Barrett of Commerce.

The affair occurred Sunday night at 7:30 o'clock, at the corner of East 10th street and Delaware Ave. The assailant, a negro, first robbed the victim after which he deliberately fired a charge from a shotgun at him, the shot lodging in Chaffin's right side. The injured man was removed to a local hospital where he died at 1:30 o'clock Monday morning.

The alleged slayer was captured early today and is being kept under cover by officers to prevent lynching, which they fear may take place.

W. A. Chaffin was married to Miss Ida Lindley of this city on December 10th. They had been home from their wedding trip only a short while. R. L. Lindley, Mrs. Chaffin's father, was notified of the shooting about ten o'clock Sunday night and left at once for Oklahoma City. Chaffin was well known to a number of people here. (*Sulphur Springs Gazette*, January 30, 1914)

W. A. CHAFFIN'S SLAYER LYNCHED BY DETERMINED BODY OF OKLAHOMA CITY MEN

Muskogee, Okla., Jan. 27.—Ben Dickerson, negro charged with the killing of W. A. Chaffin, traveling salesman at Oklahoma City, robbed and killed Sunday night, was taken from the Purcell jail at 5:30 this morning by a party in automobiles from Oklahoma City, borne to Noble, nine miles north, hanged and his body riddled with bullets. The automobile party overpowered Jailer Morgan, the only man in the Purcell jail, and took the negro without making noise enough to awaken anyone in the city.

The negro cowered in his cell and begged for mercy when the lynchers opened the doors with the jailer's keys. He protested his innocence to the last. No time or words was wasted. A rope was placed around Dickerson's neck, his hands and feet bound and he was lifted into one of the machines. This car headed the death cavalcade as it passed swiftly out of Purcell without an alarm being given and when Noble was reached the negro was strung up to the limb of a tree and his body riddled with bullets. With the body still hanging the lynchers swiftly disappeared, each auto going a different direction. The Purcell jailer gave an alarm after the mob had gone and a pursuit was started, but the pursuers were easily outdistanced by the swift machines of the lynchers. Dickerson's correct name, it is said, was Allen Mosley. He had recently been released from the Tennessee penitentiary, where he had served a term for manslaughter.

W. A. Chaffin, the negro's alleged victim was robbed and killed at Oklahoma City Sunday night. He was the son of J. H. Chaffin, a planter living near Dallas. (*Sulphur Springs Gazette*, January 30, 1914)

CHAFFIN'S SLAYER CONFESSED

Ben Dickerson, the negro lynched near Noble, Okla., Monday night made a confession which was sworn to by him before a notary public. The confession was written from statements made by the negro and does not purport to be in his exact language, but is made up of his statements. It was signed by the negro and his signature witnessed by the notary public.

"My right name is Bennie Dickerson," the negro says in the confession. "I was born at Temple, Texas, and am twenty-nine years old. I live at 613 North Georgia street in Oklahoma City with my brother-in-law James Henderson, who is a pastor of the Church of God.

On Sunday night, January 25, 1914, while my relatives were at church, I made up my mind to hold up somebody. I left my house about 7 p. m. and went north on Eighth and east to Delaware street. I went north about a fourth of a block and stopped alongside of a picket fence. This was about 7:25 o'clock, I think.

A few minutes later a man whom I have since learned was W. A. Chaffin came along wearing a light brown overcoat. I stuck the gun, a double barrel twelve-gauge Eclipse shotgun, on him and told him to hold up, which he did. I searched him and found $3.80 in money and a cheap Ingersoll watch. I made him take off his overcoat, coat and vest and did not find anything of value and threw the vest down. After searching him, I told him to go back where he came from and to keep his hands up.

When he got to the alley he turned and I turned the shotgun on him and fired one shot. I don't know whether it stuck him or not. I threw the gun down and ran south across the Katy tracks, went home and went to bed. I put the clothes under the bed. I took the diamond Elk pin off the blue coat and wrapped it in paper and put it in my pocket. This was about 10 o'clock. Shortly after my people came home from church, I asked by bother-in-law James Henderson to loan me his suitcase and grip as he did. I got up at 6:30 Monday morning January 26 and put the clothes in the grip. Iva Dickerson, my sister, made breakfast and I went down town. I tried to pawn the clothes and the diamond Elk pin at two different places, and was arrested at the last place by two officers.

I admit killing Mr. Chaffin, but I did not intend to. I was nervous and scared and afraid he was coming back to get me when I fired. I admit I have served a term in the state penitentiary in Louisiana for killing a man in a fight over some property. I served six years and seven months of an eight year sentence for killing this man. All I ask is that God will forgive me for any wrong I have done." (*Sulphur Springs Gazette*, January 30, 1914)

Sunday February 1, 1914

I stayed at home all morning. Ruth McCorkle and Ida Mae Nelson & myself went walking and went to see Ida. I had a date with E. that night. We went to the Methodist Church and after we came home. Emmet read in this diary. Believe me, I won't forget tonite. I had so much fun out of Emmet cutting up about something. "C"

Monday February 2 , 1914

I have spent the day in school. Had to stay in this evening. Too bad.

Tuesday February 3, 1914

I received two notes from Emmet today. The Little Millionaire[8] is going to be played tonight. McGee Long and Faugh & I had more fun tonite cutting up. Laura [Thornton] just phoned me and talked to me a long time.

Wednesday February 4, 1914

I went to school and studied hard tonite.

Friday February 6, 1914

O! My it has turned so cold. I almost froze in school this morning. Emmet wanted a date tonight. So he telephoned me that afternoon about 5 o'clock and I let him have date, but goodness I wished I hadn't. We did not go the Lyceum Course. Too cold to go. Something took place that nite that I don't approve of and that is not all. But I will not state here what it was but I will remember well myself never forget. I am awful sorry this occurred for I will never care for somebody as much as I did before. I was surprised. This will cause trouble but I cannot help it. I am not like some girls but I thought somebody knew it for I had told him a dozen times. I may be writing my last time of a date with Emmet Thornton for I can bear such things "C" What did he mean? I cannot understand. The first time I ever knew of him acting so ———.

Saturday February 7, 1914

My! It is so cold. Have stayed at home all day. Been in bed sick.

8 This was a 1911 musical that received great reviews when performed at the Cohan Theater in New York.

Sunday February 8, 1914

Was in bed all day long. Sick. Everybody went to Sunday school except me and I feel so bad I can barely hold up my head to write this. "C"

Saturday February 14, 1914

Johnnie Harris[9] died this afternoon at 6:00 o'clock. O my how sad. Emmet and myself, Faugh & Helen, Ruth McCorkle & McGee Long ordered flowers but they did not come.

Sunday February 15, 1914

I spent the day with Ruth McCorkle and my we had such a grand time. Directly after Sunday School we went over to Mrs. [W. P.] Harris's. Poor little Marie Quinn['s] heart [is] broken. We stayed up until 1:00 o'clock & then went to Ruth's, ate dinner and went to the station to see if our flowers come, but they did not. How disappointed I was. We then went to the funeral that evening. The High School boys were "pallbearers" and my there were so many people [that] attended. Ruth & Ida Mae Nelson & myself went. After we got home the girls came home with me and the telephone rang. It was about 5 o'clock. Was E. Wanted a date. It took a whole lot of nerve to tell him he could come but I did. So we went to church. Sister went with us to the Methodist Church.

DEATH OF JOHNNIE HARRIS

"Leaves have their time to fall.
And flowers to wither at the north wind's breath.
But thou hast all seasons for thine own,
Oh death!"

Johnnie Harris, youngest son of Mr. and Mrs. W. P. Harris of this city died at the family home

9 Johnnie H. Harris, born in 1896, was a senior classmate of Emmet.

on Saturday evening at six-thirty o'clock. Since the 4th of last August he has suffered from a complication of diseases and his parents, in the hope of relief took him to the balmy and dry air of the Rochelle country, but contrary to the habits at that section it was an unusually wet season and unfavorable for Johnnie and after some weeks, he was removed to a Sanitarium in Dallas, where he had all the care and attention that kind nursing and skillful medical service could render, but all to no avail, the disease had been at work too long and it was apparent that vital spark of life was approaching dissolution. His physician gave notice to his parents that hope had fled, and he was brought home on Thursday night prior to his death.

Johnnie was a favorite among those of his age, and one of the most affecting incidents of the funeral service was the appearance of five young men bearing the casket from the room to the waiting hearse, this their last service to their young friend was indeed touching.

Revs. J. B. Gober and Wallace Bassett conducted the funeral services at the family home on Sunday evening and interment was immediately had at the city cemetery. To the care-worn and grief-stricken parents, we send our heart felt sympathies in this sad hour of bereavement, and while their little Johnnie has passed from them, it should be comforting for them to know, his tabernacle of pain and suffering has been broken up and he has passed to the care of the "Great Physician" who can all our sorrows heal. (*Sulphur Springs Gazette*, February 16, 1914)

Friday February 20, 1914

Emmet & myself, Glynn & Beky S. & Faugh & Helen played (42) over at "Beky" S. home & my we had an awful good time.

Saturday February 21, 1914

About 3 o'clock I went to town met Kathleen and Ruth McCorkle and we bummed around town & then went to the Mission [movie] and then went home to Kathleen's & danced all afternoon. Then before supper we walked up to the Palace of Sweets & came home & ate supper then went to the Jefferson & the Lyric & after the shows we went to the Drug Store and got something to drink. G it was getting late we then went home & ate fruit till 11:30 then had music & we ragged till 12 o'clock. About this time "Kat" began to tell scary tales so we all three jumped in bed. Kat & Ruth had fixed the graphophone[10] to entertain us till we fell last asleep. Now believe me we had one more good time.

Sunday February 22, 1914

(George's Birthday) Get me. Ha! Ha! Ha! We awoke very early about—10 o'clock & rush to eat our breakfast and go to church so we dressed & went to Methodist Church. I bid the girls farewell after church and came home. Ever remember "all nite long." Tonite I had a date with Emmet & he came & we decided not to go to church. So after he had been here awhile he took a notion he wanted to go to church. So I didn't want to go but it was the first time he had ever wanted to go so we went to the Christian Church. But I am not going to please

10 The Graphophone was an improved form of the phonograph invented by Alexander Graham Bell. The name *Graphophone* was the Columbia Record version of the old phonograph.

him anymore that way (it's not fair) just this time. Kathleen and I have changed coats for a while.

Wednesday February 25, 1914

Emmet and I wanted to go to the Lyceum Course. Believe me I wanted to go but mother wouldn't let me go. This was the last one this season & I wanted to go so bad I believe if mother knew how bad I wanted to go she would let me go.

Thursday February 26, 1914

The Lyceum Course did not come last nite so E wants to go tonite, but mother still won't let me go.

Friday February 27, 1914

The B.Y.P.U. are going to have a social to-night but we are not going (I am not).

Saturday February 28, 1914

Roy C and I went to the shows and I saw somebody coming in at the Lyric Theater.

Sunday March 1, 1914

I did not go to Sunday School or church. Sunday Edith, Pauline, Jewell Cambron and Ida Mae came out to see me that afternoon. We had an awful good time playing on the piano and cutting up. I had a date that night with Emmet. He brought me the best candy. We went to church (Methodist our church) "C" Get me.

Monday March 2, 1914

There was a recital at the Methodist Church a woman read. Emmet, Grace and myself went. Had an awful good time last night. Believe me only I didn't feel good.

Thursday March 5, 1914

This is a very notable day. Emmet's birthday. It is so cold & bad. I gave him some Lanier handkerchiefs and sent them to him by Mattie Lou Ardis. He was certainly proud of them for I got the sweetest note from him (18 years old). Mother was taken very ill last night. The nurse came and is here with mother. Mrs. Mabry from Dallas. Address—1620 Pennsylvania Ave Dallas Tex. She is such a sweet woman.

Friday March 13, 1914

Today is mother's birthday and she is still sick. She got so many pretty presents.

Saturday March 14, 1914

Emmet went to Elberta Lake and brought me some of the nicest fish. Believe me they certainly were good. I certainly did think it was sweet of him to.

Sunday March 15, 1914

Today is such a pretty day not so lonesome for me. Mother is much better today. Able to be up a little. The nurse is going to leave tonite. Aunt Mattie [Birthright Mellown], Cousin Tex [Hardin], & Aunt Anna [?] is here with mother.

5

Falling in Love

"But (ish cabibble) I should worry for I had not been with him in a solid month or longer and I didn't care to go to the show but I bet he did. I mortally did enjoy his company that night for it seemed like a 100 years since he had been to see me."

As spring overshadowed winter, the warm days leaped forward to revitalize the weathered teenagers. Back to school, fun dates, and a May Day festival all intertwined to bring Emmet and Alma closer together.

Monday March 16, 1914

I went back to school today and certainly was glad to get back to. Have been out a week.

Friday March 20, 1914

Emmet wanted a date with me, but he could not come. Mother was not well enough.

Sunday March 22, 1914

Emmet phoned and wanted a date but he could not come. My, just think he did not come last Sunday and is not coming tonight. I retired at 9 o'clock. Emmet phoned me and talked to me a long time. My, I was so mad because he could not come.

Friday March 27, 1914

This has been such a dreadful day for me. E. wanted a date tonight but I could not let him come.

Saturday March 28, 1914

I had just completed my bath and began to dress when Emmet came to take me car riding. We took Kathleen and Ruth McCorkle and we went all over town. My! I enjoyed it so much. He ask for a date but I did not let him have it.

Friday April 3, 1914

Murphy's comedians[1] are here and Emmet and I had planned to go but it was unrelenting rain and therefore we didn't get to go. But (ish cabibble) I should worry for I had not been with him in a solid month or longer and I didn't care to go to the show but I bet he did. I mortally did enjoy his company that night for it seemed like a 100 years since he had been to see me. I got a little bit mad but not much at him finally I got in a good humor. It was not my fault though.

Sunday April 5, 1914

The Baptist meeting started today. So E and Ego came out to see Nellie [?] and I. We went to the church but got there to late so we came back home. Now, believe me I felt good after E. left. He promised me he would never mention something to me again, and he meant it to. I know. Maybe you think I am not tickled.

Monday April 6, 1914

I got two notes from E. today. They were cute to. They get sweeter all the time to me. He and I have just about quit fussing unless he is the cause of it then I have to fuss a little. Don't want to do it but he makes me.

---

1 Murphy's Comedians were famous as an acting group doing their vaudeville performances in many small US towns. The prices for a ticket at their engagements were ten cents for general admission and twenty-five cents to obtain reserved seating. The Comedians not only performed in a community, they competed with local athletes in various contest including extremely competitive baseball games. After finishing in Sulphur Springs, Murphy's Comedians moved west with performances the following days in Commerce and Sherman, Texas.

Tuesday April 7, 1914

I got a note from E. early and he talked so sweet about something, something that I have been worrying over a long time, but dare not mention it to him. He has decided to do something that would do me more good. O! how I wish he would. He asked me for a date to go to church with him tonight, and just think it turned so cold that I could not go. I wonder why it did that way for I wanted to go with him so bad. So think that he really ask me to go. I will not forget something as long as I live. No, never. I hope now he will go tonight and enjoy it just as much as if I was sitting by his side. Never mind. Maybe someday real soon, I can go with him. Perhaps it won't be so cold. I will do my best tonight & I expect I can do as much or more for him then if I were at church with him. I am alone now, and will stop writing tonite.

Friday April 10, 1914

The juniors of S.S.H.S. entertained the seniors at Mrs. Ponders. We had such a nice time but I was so sick that night I could hardly hold up my head. I went with Emmet, and everyone seemed to have such a nice time.

Sunday April 12, 1914

I had a date with Emmet and we went to church at the Methodist Church.

Monday April 13, 1914

I went to church and Emmet came home with me. Will never forget that night after we got home. I felt so good. "C"

Wednesday April 15, 1914

Nona Williams, Gussie Gordon, Mildred Wood, Jimmie Wester, Emmet and myself went car riding after school and had so much fun. Will never forget all the little things that happened that evening "(The Farm)"

Friday April 17, 1914

"Within the Law"[2] was played. Emmet and I went. It was so good. I enjoyed it so much.

Sunday April 19, 1914

I had a date with Emmet and we went to church. Ruth McCorkle ate supper with me and we all went to the Methodist Church.

Tuesday April 21, 1914

Ever remember this day as long as I live, for I told someone a little secret I had been keeping away from him a long, long, long time. Believe me I could not help from telling him. I wonder if he cared anything about me telling him. I expect he did. I had such funny feeling all day that day. My, just think he brought me a pretty red rose that day it was so pretty and that rose meant more to me than any rose I ever expect to wear. "C" O! My how good I feel tonight. Wish I could see someone.

Friday April 24, 1914

I had a date with E. and it rained and rained until late and did not go anywhere. Stayed at home. I will always remember tonight.

Sunday April 26, 1914

I went to Sunday School and did not stay for church. Emmet walked home with me and stayed a little while and about 1 o'clock, Ida Mae Nelson came by to take me car riding.

---

2 *Within the Law* was a play by Bayard Veiller which was performed more than five hundred times at the Empire Theater in New York from September 1912 to December 1913.

We did not go for it began raining. So I spent most of the afternoon with Ida Mae. Emmet phoned me that night and talked with me. I kinda got a little angry that night at him and I won't forget a few things he said that night.

Monday April 27, 1914

Went to school early. Talked to E. before school. He brought me a pretty rose.

Tuesday April 28, 1914

I went to town that afternoon and Emmet, Nona and myself went to the show. Had more fun.

Wednesday April 29, 1914

Faugh and myself went to the show. Had more fun.

Thursday April 30, 1914

Went to school real early help decorate the high school float. That day I got a little vexed at Emmet. He made me mad. That afternoon Ollie and Mary Prim from Commerce came for May Day. I went home after they came and we went to town and Jimmie and Emmet came home with us. We had so much fun that night. Emmet brought Able Pate and Roy Lundy out to see the girls and we did not go anywhere it rained too bad.

Friday May 1, 1914

This morning is so pretty for May Day. I was on the High School float got first prize. We girls went to town about 1:15 and met Emmet and Mary Connally and we went car riding and went nearly to Cumby. My, I will never forget this afternoon. I run the car a little. Just learning how. We had so much fun at Brasher about buying "cold drinks." We were coming home and happen to a little accident. Got ditched. My I was scared to death. Believe me but Emmet wasn't I don't think. He didn't act like he was. We were pulled out by Tom Riley Lindley. I sure was glad to get back to town. Believe me. That night Emmet brought Drue [Connally] and Eugene Hinnant out to see the girls. We went to the show. Had so much fun that night.

MAY DAY FESTIVAL A GREAT SUCCESS; RECORD-BREAKING CROWD IN ATTENDANCE

May 1st, 1914, will go down in history as one of the biggest days Sulphur Springs ever witnessed in all the years of the town's existence up to that date. The fact that the attraction which brought the people here was furnished entirely by home people and without the aid of any out-side agency whatever makes the event of still greater importance to our citizenship. Fully fifteen thousand people participated in the May Day celebration and witnessed the parade and other activities of the day, according to estimates made by the judges.

To attempt to describe in detail the beauty and originality of the various floats and decorations in the parade would be to essay a task that must be so evidently impossible to all who witnessed the event, that it cannot be expected. With the memory of last year's notable successful May Day demonstration still fresh in the minds of all, it was somewhat of a task to get up anything that would surpass that event in point of beauty and artistic effect, yet there is hardly a one who will not admit that this year the parade and general program was even superior to the first one a year ago.

Many of the merchants and owners of autos, profiting by the experience gained thru last years' decorating, thought up schemes and carried out plans of decorations that made their efforts of a year ago seem to suffer by comparison. What may be done when they have had two or three years' experience can only be conjectured.

When the long line of floats, autos and livestock exhibits finally started toward the square from the assembly place at the Cotton Belt depot, it reached the entire distance and then some. There were many more different features this year to take a place in the parade. One of the most noteworthy of the new entries was the horseback parade and livestock exhibit of Bob Phillips and others. Floats from other places in the county were in the parade also, notably the one from Hatchetsville representing a general merchandise store at that place.

The day was so full and so crowded with the different events that there is considerable talk of making it a two day affair next year.

Too much praise cannot be given the members of the Waverly Club for their untiring effort to establish and carry to successful culmination an annual event of so great magnitude and of such widespread popularity and enthusiastic acceptance.

Henceforth May Day shall be a red letter day on the Sulphur Springs calendar. Always shall the citizens of the town and county celebrate the coming of spring with parades and various festival activities.

Alma in the May Day Parade

Introductory to the ceremony of crowning the queen, Hon. L. E. Gee, our newly-installed mayor, made a short speech of welcome and optimistic congratulation and prophecy.

After the crowning of the queen, Miss Kathleen Williams, by the first maid of honor, Miss Hazel Ripley, the "Royal Float" led the parade off past the judge's stand where the awards were made. (*Sulphur Springs Gazette*, May 8, 1914)

Saturday May 2, 1914

We spent the day with Miss Jessie Butler and it rained all afternoon. So we retired easy street night at 8 o'clock.

Sunday May 3, 1914

We all went to Sunday School and to the Baptist Church. Emmet went with us and nearly walked home with. The girls went home this afternoon. Believe me there was a big crowd at the station. Emmet and myself and Ruth (she ate dinner with us) with Ida Mae and we had so much fun. I forgot and did something this afternoon I'm not going to do anymore on Sunday—no I'm not—for it isn't nice—but—just think who else did it too. I don't care. We won't do it anymore. I am sitting here now by myself fixing to go to sleep. I don't have any date to-night. I am so glad. I am so sleepy.

Friday May 8, 1914

I went to town Friday afternoon and met Emmet. Brought me home and carried us for a little drive that night. I had a date with him and we went to the Jefferson Theater[3] and then went to the B.Y.P.U. party at Mrs. James. We came back to town with Hazel R. and Edith B. and we all went to the Palace of Sweets, then went back to the party. Had such a good time. Emmet and I came home that night by ourselves, but the moon was shining so pretty. I surely did have a good time.

Sunday May 10 1914

I went to Sunday School. Emmet went with me. Wasn't that sweet of him. I think so. We all think so. Then we went to church and he came home with me. About 2 o' clock he phoned me and he came out about 3, and we went car riding. Went to Cumby. Believe me I surely did enjoy the drive that time. Came home about 6 o' clock and I had a date with him to go to church that night. He came kinder late but luck would have it McGee L. came along in the car and we went to church with him in the car. My I was so sleepy that night I could hardly hold my eyes open, but Emmet tried his best to keep me awake. But it was all he could do to try. We were so tired when we got home that night I could hardly walk any farther.

---

3 The Jefferson Theatre was billed as one of the most elegant and complete opera houses outside of the larger cities to be found in the state. The house had a gallery, parquet, dress circle, and orchestra pit. It featured one of the largest stages in the state, great height for scenery, with ample side and rear stage room. During the summer, moving pictures were shown, always with "splendid music at each performance" (*Sulphur Springs Gazette*, September 12, 1913).

6
Best of Times

"I saw someone, he looked so manly and bold walking down that isle. He will never look that way again to me for he was so brave. This morning has been the happiest day I ever spent."

Although extremely active, Sulphur Springs Christians dotted but a small spot on the landscape of what eventually became known as the Bible Belt. Located on the western end of this religious region, adults and teenagers centered their Sunday schedules socially and spiritually on what each church provided.

In the white section of the city, there were six primary churches. Emmet attended the Baptist Church, whose $35,000 structure made it the most expensive of the religious buildings. Just behind them was the Methodist Church built for $20,000. "Comfortable and roomy" were the Presbyterian Church, the Catholic Church, and the Episcopalian Church. Striving to increase attendance, the Christian Church was in the process of building a church house valued at $15,000.

Alma's family were members of the Methodist Church and rarely missed Sunday school, morning church service, or the evening session. Tracing her strong belief in Christ back to this time, Alma became the longest living active member of the First United Methodist Church in the mid-1990s.

Sunday, particularly when the season was agreeable, was easily the hub of a young person's week. Activities started early and lasted deep into the evening. Although an individual's religious denomination ranked foremost for parents, not so for teenagers. The parameters for their attendance at a church service, more than occasionally, were to follow friends to different meetings to obtain what they craved above all else, exciting social interaction.

Friday May 15, 1914

My today was such a pretty day. We had planned to go on a picnic tomorrow but have decided differently. "C" Winnsboro is going to play ball here this afternoon. (S.S.H.S. Boys) got beat.[1] The telephone rang about 4 o'clock and it was Emmet, and what do you think I could not hear him at all. But "C" he went & phoned me where I could hear him. (I don't forget [these] little deeds). I let him have a date and we went to church, Lockett Adair[2] and came home. I went to sleep. Had the awfullest dreams about (someone) killing me. My! It was scary and exciting. I will not relate it here though for it is too awful. Yes yes.

GREAT REVIVAL NOW IN PROGRESS: LOCKETT ADAIR DRAWS LARGE CROWDS

The revival meeting which has been in progress at the Coliseum since Thursday night of last week, is gathering force and strength as the days go by. Lockett Adair is a great evangelist: he doesn't cling to the time-honored classical or theological style of preaching and doesn't care how much he butchers the "King's English" he is preaching to lost souls and he doesn't care what method he uses in reaching their hearts and convincing them of the error of their way. He possesses the God-given power of commanding attention: he strikes sledge-hammer blows that are destined to smash the crust over the most hardened and calloused

1 Sulphur Springs lost the game 4–3.

2 Benjamin Lockett Adair was a famous Christian evangelist. The *Sulphur Springs Gazette* said "Lockett Adair is a living example that whoever will may come! From a drunkard, a gambler, a spendthrift and a reprobate he has been transformed to one of the strongest and most highly successful evangelist in the Southwest, all through the religion of Jesus Christ" (June 12, 1914).

> heart; his message goes home; the sinner is forced to a realization of his lost condition; some times the sinner comes home at once but often he battles against that "still small voice" which cries out to him "come home, come home;" but Lockett Adair's force and power is such that a soul convicted of its sins cannot stand the strain long, complete submission finally comes and the sinner comes home to God. (*Sulphur Springs Gazette*, May 22, 1914)

Saturday May 16. 1914

I stayed at home all day. It rained all day long, but I made my first cake.

Sunday May 17, 1914

I got up and went to Sunday School & somebody & me went to church & somebody walked part of the way home with me. He phoned about 2:20 that afternoon and I went to the girls meeting and he went to the boys meeting then we met "C" and came on home then. We went to church that night and it began raining so we came home before church was over. Sister went with us and we had a good time when we got home. But I was a little sleepy so "good nite to all."

Monday May 18, 1914

Got up early and went to school and saw somebody there. I stayed at school all day and got two the sweetest notes I ever expect to receive. That morning Mrs. Stover and Mr. Stover[3]

---

3 Mr. F. R. Stover was the director of the choir for the Adair Revival. His wife was a featured singer who drew splendid reviews for her solos. The *Sulphur Springs Gazette* noted "The Stover's are musicians of the first class and are recipients of gratitude and praise" (May 22, 1914). They also conducted afternoon services with Mr. Stover meeting with the men and Mrs. Stover with the women.

came out to school and entertained us. That evening Emmet came out to get his invitations & stamp them so we stamped them & had more fun. Yes we did. That night I went to church and who did I see on the corner but a little companion to go to church with me as we went. Mattie McCauley, Sister & Miss Vera [McCauley] went too and when we came home. I wasn't a bit sleepy but wrote in this little book that tells the truth & nothing else.

Tuesday May 19, 1914

I went to school and someone had brought me two pretty roses—one "white" and one "red" one. I went to church that night with Sister, Miss Mattie and Miss Vera. Did not see anyone but I bet he was there.

Wednesday May 20, 1914

Went to school real early that morning but no one did I see. So I studied real hard, for a long time until someone came. Brought me a pretty rose. This was white. About 2:20 I got a note asking me to come to town to help him mail his invitations. My, I felt so bad, but for somebody I went to town and I walked around town and nobody was to be seen. Went to see the "Mutual Girl"[4] and came home. I shall not relate here my thoughts & feelings but I shall never forget. Don't believe I could ever forget them. That night I went to church with Mrs. W. McCauley in their car and met somebody on the way and saw somebody as he was going in home that night with a crowd of boys. Yes, he had been to church. I know, I wonder, what thoughts he was having & I know the ones I was having. Well I am sleepy and will quit & stop these bad thoughts.

4 *Our Mutual Girl* was a fifty-two-weekly, one-reel episode, starring Norma Phillips as the Mutual Girl. The action/romantic series ran in theaters from January 1914 to January 1915.

Thursday May 21, 1914

I went to school and got there about 9 o'clock. Received a note from Emmet. O! that note & he sent me a rose. It was red but no, not by the same feeling the little "red" rose was sent. I wouldn't wear the old rose no, I wouldn't. It shattered in just a little while. I wrote Emmet and told him just how I had felt & how I felt then. Got an answer but it did not suit me. That night I went to church.

Friday May 22, 1914

(Received my last note) Today is a day that I have longed to come for the past two days. Emmet wrote and ask for a date and I let him have one for I had something to tell him. Important. He came early and we went to the Lyric and from there we went to the Place of Sweets & there went the Jefferson Theater "C" Fought tonight. Just think about it. Emmet would not even talk to me at the Jefferson. He had something on his mind that was worrying him, but I don't know what it was. Wish I did know what it was that was on his mind. I asked him something & he didn't ever answer me. I never spent such a miserable night in my life I don't believe. Coming home that night I could not say a word. I couldn't. I was not the cause of it. I know if I was I don't know how. When we got home, Emmet told me something I can't believe it but he said it. If I only knew he meant it I would be a different girl altogether to think someone cares for (me).

Saturday May 23, 1914

I stayed at home all morning got a card from one of the girls in Commerce that she was coming on the evening train so I met her and we went to town and we met Emmet. We all went to the show and then went car riding. I don't know what I would do if it weren't for Emmet to help me show the girls a nice time. Then Saturday night we went to church and someone was sitting at the court house waiting for a tacky little gal to go to church with him. So we all went to church and came home for I was so sleepy & tired.

Sunday May 24, 1914

We got up real early and dressed. Lee [?] and myself went to the cemetery and carried the pretty flowers she brought me. We came home and got ready and went to Sunday School, but got there to late so we went on down to the Tabernacle and Emmet came down there and we went from there to the Christian Church where they having their dedication of their church but we got there too late and we came on home. That afternoon at train time we just did get to the train in time. Emmet and Drue were down there and Emmett and I went over to Ruth's and spent the afternoon. We all started home and came through town and then on out home. The girls and Emmet walked nearly to the railroad with me then they went back. I studied that night about a minute then went to sleep after Emmet phoned.

Monday May 25, 1914

Examinations begin this morning. My how I dread to take them. They last till Thursday.

Friday May 29, 1914

Emmet phoned me but it was raining and he couldn't come. So I went to sleep real early last night.

Saturday May 30, 1914

I sent the girls their graduating presents this morning. Am being real smart and am fixing to cook a good cake for mother.

Sunday May 31, 1914

I went to the cemetery real early & came home & got ready and went to Sunday School and today they preached the

(Baccalaureate) Sermon for the Seniors. After Sunday School we went to the Baptist Church. After church I came home and it wasn't long till the telephone rang. It was Emmet. He came out that night & honest I never did enjoy his company any more than that night. We stayed at home. That night did not go to church. I gave him a little graduating present, a little brush. It wasn't much but was enough to let him know I thought of him.

Monday June 1, 1914

This month has rolled around so fast. Just think this time last year how I felt and how I feel this year about someone. The seniors have Class Day today at the High School. Emmet read his essay.[5] Read it real good. I was real proud of him. Yes I was. Wish I was finishing with him this year. I served punch in the Serving Room where we had our Serving Exhibit. I got my card and passed (to the 11th grade. I was so glad I passed.) The graduating exercise was at the Opera House. All the class looked so pretty. Our class were ushers. There were so many pretty flowers given to the boys and girls. Emmet came home with me that night. We came by his home and put his flowers up, then we came on home. good-nite.

SIXTEEN GRADUATE FROM SULPHUR SPRINGS HIGH SCHOOL

The program at the Jefferson Theatre Monday night by the members of the 1914 graduating class of the Sulphur Springs High School marked the close of a splendid series of exercises which it has been the privilege of our people to enjoy the past few days.

5 Each member of the graduating class were required to write an essay or an oration of not fewer than one thousand words to be approved by the high school faculty and superintendent before graduation. This counted as one-half of the grade in English for the final semester of school.

The program Monday morning was given at the High School building and the auditorium was filled with friends of the graduates and the city schools. After an introductory speech by Prof. Haynie, the following program was rendered.

Piano Solo—Miss Carrie Rogers
Essay—"Friendship""—Miss Mattie Lou Artis
"Texas Our Biggest State"—Ben Buford
Music—Maggie Sherwood
Essay—"Orator"—Tom Sid Gafford
Essay—"Thought"—Will Southerland
Music—Miss Nona Williams
Essay—"Home Economies—Miss Laverne Patrick
Song—"Childhood Dreams"—Miss Mattie Lou Ardis
Essay—"Agriculture"—Emmet Thornton
Essay—"Athletics"—Glynn Pickett
Music—Miss Ruth Hicks

Hon. Dozier Thornton, always prepared to bring a message of cheer and hopefulness to young hearts as well as old, made a short talk on the reward of labor and expressed himself as confident of the continued growth and betterment of our city schools. He commended the faithfulness of the teachers and the unselfish rendering of their services for the final week of school when the funds were exhausted and they gave their time and teaching without money and without price.

Monday night the crowning feature of the presentation of the exercises took place at the Jefferson Theatre with diplomas. After the invocation by Rev. R. C. Hicks, the members of the class arose and joined in the welcome chorus.

The Salutatorian Miss Carrie Rogers, with her sweet, modest voice read an essay on the importance of grasping the opportunities of the living present and not, like our Mexican neighbors, living always in a land of "manna" or tomorrow.

The Valedictory by Miss Marie Quinn expressed regret at the necessity for the breaking of the ties which bound the class members together during the four years of High School, but voiced the hope that the associations that had been theirs during that time might remain in their memories to be cherished and to brighten life's pathway.

As a preface to the presentation of the diplomas, Hon. D. Thornton, president of the Board of Trustees, announced that the Superintendent of city schools received a letter yesterday stating that, because of certain points of excellence which have been maintained in our high school, our affiliation with the State University of Texas has been strengthened another point. This was the best of news and the announcement was cheered heartily. The exercises closed with the Commencement song, sung by the class. (*Sulphur Springs Gazette*, June 5, 1914)

Tuesday June 2, 1914

Today I am so sleepy I hardly know what to do. The boys Roy and Glynn are going home with Faugh. The seniors are going

Class of 1914 (front) *La Verne Patrick, Nona Williams, Mary Cummings, Marie Quinn, Mattie Lou Ardis, Carrie Rogers, and Maggie Sherwood;* (second row) *Tom Sid Gafford, Roy Caldwell, Lillie Leach, Ruth Hicks, Jimmy Wester, and Billy Southerland;* (back) *E. A. Haynie (principal), Glynn Pickett, and Emmet Thornton. Ben Buford missed the picture.*

to have their pictures made today. I hope they will and Emmet will be in it and then I will have a picture of him. "C" We went to church that night. The McCauley girls and myself and nobody did I "c" until I saw him come out of a moving picture show. I had been to church. Jimmie Wester walked home with me that night. Tomorrow morning all the old Seniors of S.S. H. S. are going to have a moonshine breakfast out at the "Reservoir." I wish I was a Senior ! "C"

Wednesday June 3, 1914

At las'. Since the boys left I have my room back again fixed cute. I am so proud of it. I dressed real early and we went to church. Emmet came home with me that night and his arm was hurting him so bad where he had had the Serum used. I know it did. Yes it did.

Friday June 5, 1914

Got up real early and I wrote 2 letters. Then after dinner I went to sleep and had not been asleep a minute it seemed to me until someone again woke me up. It was Emmet had come to stay a little while with me. He was going to take the little gal car riding but her Mother thought best for her not to go. He stayed till 5:30 and I let him have a date that night. We went to church then came back through town & _________. Emmet was sporting a pretty ruby ring, believe me it was good looking. My! I had such a good time that night!

Saturday June 6, 1914

Today is Saturday. My this week has seemed like ages to me, a month. Ruth and Annie Mae Sellers came over to the house early and they stayed till about 5:30 then we went driving. Went through town & saw Emmet & talked to him a little while. I am sitting here fixing to go to sleep so will say "good night."

Sunday June 7, 1914

I went to Sunday School to the tabernacle and Ruth wanted me to spend the day with her in which I did. So we stayed for church, went to the choir. Today the meeting closed and when Adair was begging for those to come something told me somebody was coming so as I looked up I saw someone, he looked so manly and bold walking down that isle. He will never look that way again to me for he was so brave. This morning has been the happiest day I ever spent. His father also came behind him. My how good that sounded to me. Emmet walked home with us and I had a headache so bad I could hardly see. Emmet rang me about 2 o'clock—1 minute after and talked with me. I had just begun to think about going home when Emmet came up in the car. We went and got Una Melton and a girl visiting her from Greenville and we all went to Brashear &

Cumby. I have a date with Emmet tonight. We went to church and we both enjoyed it so much. To think no longer did he feel as he had & no longer did I feel about him as I had before. We both felt good and enjoyed the services. "C" good night.

> **THE GREAT REVIVAL CLOSED-TWO HUNDRED SIXTY FOUR CONVERSIONS**
>
> Evangelist Lockett Adair closed the greatest revival meeting ever conducted in Sulphur Springs, last Sunday night, with the greatest service ever held here, after having delivered a masterful and appealing sermon on: "Why I Belong to the Church." His sermon was pronounced a gem of force and eloquence, and his congregation was deeply stirred. Thirty-six conversions were had and the service continued over 'till twelve o'clock.
>
> There are some scenes that beggar description of tongue or pen, and this was one of those rare occasions! There hardened sinners laid bare their souls and made the start for higher and better things; there innocent young manhood and young womanhood took up the Cross of the Galilean and entered upon the vista of religious duty; there strong men and women wept through sheer joy and it seemed that God and all his angels had come down to electrify and bless the closing service of this great meeting. (*Sulphur Springs Gazette*, June 12, 1914)

Monday June 8, 1914

We are taking house cleaning. My how I dread it. Well it is 11:20. Emmet has just left and has not been gone long. He came up in the car just about the time I was fixing to go to work. My,

Mattie Ruth Caldwell

what good news he brought me. Said his mother went up last night. My how good that makes me feel to think Emmet perhaps has been the cause of his father and mother turning

Tuesday June 9, 1914

Ruth and I are going to Commerce tomorrow. I am real busy today getting ready. About 3:30, Emmet came out to see. Laura brought him in the car. He stayed till they came after him. Ruth came in the buggy and we went to town. Emmet went to Brasher that afternoon with a boasting crowd (O.U.B.). Ruth brought me home early. Emmet brought me some of the prettiest flowers. They were so pretty—pink ones. Mattie Ruth came back from Dallas today. My I was glad to see her. Believe me.

Wednesday June 10, 1914

Ruth came over here real early and just before train time Emmet came in the car to carry us to the station. My! How I hated to leave—the first time in a year to leave <u>someone</u> to stay away awhile. We reached Commerce about 4 o'clock and Ollie and Mary and Edgar Brigance and Lawrence Sparkman met us. We were so glad to "C" each other. We went by the Palace of Sweets and got something to drink. Then went out home. Wednesday nite we girls went to the show. <u>About 9 & 9:30 I looked a the clock. Emmet was baptized.</u> I will never forget the first night "(<u>He joined the Baptist Church</u>)." In Commerce at 10:30 o'clock Leslie [Clifton] had not left so Ollie & I went to bed & left Mary

& Ruth to entertain him. That night Hort Newman & all we girls went to the Palace of Sweets to get something to drink. I slept so good that night.

Thursday June 11, 1914

We girls got up real early & went to town and I saw nearly all my old friends. I wrote a letter last night & sent it to someone, but didn't get a letter from him this morning. Maybe I will this afternoon. I mailed 16 cards this morning to Sulphur Springs. We went home to dinner & after dinner the girls came over and we all went to town. Had so much fun that afternoon. The first place I went to was the post office & got a great big letter. Yes I did from somebody too. Thursday night I wrote him a long letter. Yes I did and we went to town to mail it & went to the show.

Friday June 12, 1914

We had planned to go on a big picnic today. The boys got the big float & there was 21 in all that went. The following went—Claude Young, Mr. Mycle, Reeves Fuller, Karl Hendrix, Lester Jackson, Leslie Clifton, Mr. Lester Dewitt, Mr. Drake, Grace and Pauline Hayslip, the 3 Mauldin girls and Loyola DeVaney, & Miss Brown and Mrs. Utley and Mary, Ollie, Ruth, Annie Bachman & myself. We started about 8:30.

Had such a good time going. We ate our dinner at 12 o'clock. Dewitt asking the blessing & Mrs. Utley & I spread dinner. After eating we went fishing and made 2 dozen Kodak pictures. Around 3:30 there was quite a little accident happened. Karl fell from the grape vine swing. It broke with him. My, I thought for a while he was dead. We soon had him up able to make the picture. "C"

We started home about 6 o'clock. Ollie & I came home with Annie & Mr. Drake. My that drive home in a buggy was nice to me. Just as I got out of the buggy to go in the house, Rose (Ollie's little sister) came running to me with a big box & a letter from home. I thought at first it was something mother had sent me but upon opening I found it was some of the prettiest red roses & pink & white ones Emmet had sent me "C" and a great big letter. My how good I did feel even if I had been on a picnic. That reminded me. Made me feel good to think that someone had thought enough of me, even if he had gone to write me a long letter & even send me some red roses. That proves to me, yes it does. That night we dressed and Herbert Wheeler came out to the house with the bunch. I had written Emmet a long letter, so we went to town & mailed it at the hotel so we thought he would be sure & get it. We went back home by the drug store & saw Mattie Lou & several Sulphur Springs friends of ours. I slept good that night to think you would be there the next night.

Saturday June 13, 1914

I got up early & I went to visit all the old friends, my old neighbors & all. They all look good to me & I got a letter. We ate dinner that day with Gertrude. A 3:40 we met the train. Guess who came. Emmet & Lou Ada on that train. My! I was so glad to see them. They looked good to me. We went the show that afternoon. Then went home. That night we went to the Chautauqua.[6] I don't believe I ever enjoyed Emmet's company any more than I did then. (good nite)

CHAUTAUQUA IS A SUCCESS

The success of the Commerce Chautauqua (first ever) now bids fair to exceed the expectations of all parties concerned, in both interest and attendance. Every number on the program so

6 Chautauqua was a group of speakers, entertainers, and preachers who traveled through the rural United States (competing with the Lyceum movement) bringing culture, entertainment, and ideas to the various areas. Founded in 1874 on the banks of Chautauqua Lake in the state of New York by a Methodist minister John Heyl Vincent and businessman Lewis Miller, it remained a powerful motivating and educational force until the middle of the 1920s. They held their performances, usually lasting a week, in their own facility (a huge tent called a *tabernacle*). The Commerce Chautauqua was a five-day affair.

far has proved highly pleasing. The hours of the meetings have been changed to 3:00 in the afternoon and 8 o'clock at night. Following is the programs yet to come:

Saturday night: The Old Home Singers, Ralph Parlette, humorous lecturer[7]
Sunday afternoon: The Italian Marine Band, Ned Woodman, cartoonist
Sunday night: The Italian Band, Sermon
(*Commerce Journal*, June 19, 1914)

Sunday June 14, 1914

We all went to Sunday School & from there out to Mary & Ollie's where we all ate dinner. We went to the station. Annie Bachman & Mr. Drake & Herbert Wheeler went with us. My, I was so glad I decided to come home today for I wanted to come with someone. Herbert came home with Ruth. When we got home Annie Mae Sellers and Robert Hicks met us all. We all came up home & stayed till the next train for Herbert to go back. No, he wouldn't stay over.

After we went to the station and came home, Emmet came home with me & stayed until 5:30. (I gave him something) "C" He wanted a date but I was so sleepy. I didn't want him to leave me. I told him I would go to sleep & so I did. I couldn't help it, no I couldn't. He left about 9:30. I was so sleepy. I enjoyed his company but I was sleepy. He knew it too. He brought me 2 of the prettiest roses & a great, great Big Nice picture of himself in the graduating class (something that I have longed for ever since we have been going together.) He brought me 2. I don't know which I think the most of. It is hard to tell. I know though.

7 Ralph Parlette, the humorist Alma watched perform, was emerging as a respected author for his 1914 publication of a book titled *The University of Hard Knocks*, which he would lecture from more than 2,500 times during the Chautauqua and Lyceum tours.

June 14, 1914

Monday June 15, 1914

I went to town and saw somebody & talked with him a long time. Yes I did.

Tuesday June 16, 1914

I stayed at home all day. Have been in bed sick all day & someone phoned me and talked a long time how much better I did feel after he phoned.

Good Friends: Maggie Sherwood, Marie Quinn, Mamie Rash, and Mattie Lou Artis

Wednesday June 17, 1914

A year ago today I began going with Emmet. We have been going together pretty regular, and have spent some of the happiest hours & days I ever spent. I hope all the years of my life will be spent as happy as these were. This year has passed the quickest of any year I ever spent. My. Remember a year today & to-night. Tonight.

June 17/ 14

One year ago tonight this nobody came to see (for the first time) some little girl. She was so good, so kind, so sweet to a poor sorry fellow like me. This old mostly friendship toward some sweet little girl soon grew into "LOVE." An because some little girl was kind enough to return a little love has made this the happiest man in the world.

E.T.

7
Love Everlasting

"His philosophy of life was a thing of esthetic beauty in its child-like simplicity. He lived for two things: his family and his profession; he knew but two places his home and his office."

Two weeks later, while Alma and Emmet enjoyed the fruits of courtship, the world plunged into World War I. The assassination of Archduke Franz Ferdinand of Austria, the heir to the throne of Austria–Hungry, ignited the spark, which would extinguish the lives of 116,708 young Americans and wound 205,690 others by 1918.

The romance of Emmet and Alma never waned despite the presence of a war or Emmet pursuing a law degree. He passed the state bar exam with ease and on April 23, 1915, and he became the youngest practicing attorney in the state of Texas. With a bubbling excitement for his new profession obvious to all, he joined his father at the age of nineteen to create the Thornton and Thornton law firm located on the southeast corner of the town square in Sulphur Springs.

Alma 1915

The year 1915 found Alma finishing her education at Sulphur Springs High School in June and marrying "someone" on her favorite day—December 23. The two lovebirds—he a more-than-charming new hometown attorney and she, a beautiful but spirited young woman—were married at Alma's home. Tom Ramey served as Best Man, and

Emmet 1915

Lou Ada Caldwell was the Matron of Honor. Following the ceremony,

> "We toured to the city and had supper at the café, after which we were entertained at the Buford Theater (good night)!"

Alma became a mother and homemaker for the expanding Thornton family, and Emmet took off on a sky rocketing career. In 1917, the voters elected him city attorney for Sulphur Springs, and in

Mrs. Dr. L. W. Caldwell
requests the honor of your presence at the marriage
of her daughter
Alma Weeks
to
Mr. Emmet Thornton
Thursday evening, December the twenty-third
nineteen hundred and fifteen
at seven-thirty o'clock
at her home, nine hundred and thirty-three Davis street
Sulphur Springs, Texas

December 23, 1915

Carolyn, Dozier, Mary and Martha Lou

the coming years, the electorate selected him as the county attorney of Hopkins County for four consecutive terms. He voluntarily retired in 1931 to return to private practice. Despite many requests to do so, he never entertained running for public office again.

A year after their marriage, the couple celebrated the birth of a son Dozier and in the following thirteen years, three daughters, Martha Lou, Mary Jean, and Carolyn. Emmet became the perfect father for the fast-growing household despite working long hours to keep the family financially sound during a time of hardship for the United States—the Great Depression.

In 1941, after living east of town on College Road RD 5, the Thornton family moved into their new dream home at 955 North Davis Street, a scant hundred yards north of Alma's mother's house. They lived here happily married until the tragic day of Monday, April 6, 1942, when Emmet, while at home, had a heart attack and left his family behind. It was devastating to all those who loved and respected him.

After his untimely death, the local newspaper wrote many, many things about Emmet and his accomplishments. One such paragraph summed up his love of job and family.

955 North Davis St.

> [His] philosophy of life was a thing of esthetic beauty in its child-like simplicity. He lived for two things: his family and his profession; he knew but two places his home and his office. He was unaffected and uninfluenced by modern intricacies of life, deriving pleasure from his family, and was justly proud of its members. (*Sulphur Springs Daily News-Telegram*, April 6, 1942)

There is no higher honor for a faithful, loving husband and father than the preceding words.

Alma continued with life raising her family alone, abstaining from marriage and never moving from the home Emmet built for her. She had lost her one and only love, but his memory remained with her forever. In 1998, when the time came for her to leave this world, she went to meet her Maker from the same earthly spot as her husband, 955 North Davis Street. She was 101.

Sulphur Springs, Texas—Five generations of Alma's family in a picture taken at her beloved 955 North Davis Street home. Front row: *Alma "Mama" Thornton (1896), great granddaughter Amy Pearce McInnis (1969), great-great granddaughter Grayson McInnis (1997).* Back row: *daughter Mary Jean Thornton Pearce (1926) and grandson John Pearce (1947)*

Bibliography

Books

Espejo, Roman. *The Age of Reform and Industrialization 1896–1920 Volume 6*. Farmington Hills, Michigan: Greenhaven Press, 2003.

Fleming, E. B. *Early History of Hopkins County, Texas*. S.P., 1902.

Owens, William A. *This Stubborn Soil*. New York: Charles Scribner's Sons, 1966.

———. *A Season of Weathering*. New York: Charles Scribner's Sons, 1971.

Wukovits, John F. *The 1910's*. San Diego, California: Greenhaven Press, Inc., 2000.

The Grolier Library of World War I :The Causes of the War. Danbury, Connecticut: Grolier Publishing Company, Inc, 1997.

The 20th Century Day by Day. Millennium. New York: DK Publishing Inc, 1999.

Our American Century End of Innocence 1910–1920. Alexandria, Virginia: Time-Life Book, 2000.

Magazines

National Geographic, Volume XXIV December 1913.

Texas Almanac State Industrial Guide, 1936.

Newspapers

Commerce Journal

Sulphur Springs Gazette

Sulphur Springs Daily News Telegram

Wichita Daily Times (Wichita Falls, Texas)

High School Annuals/Programs/Guides

Graduating Exercises Commerce High School June, 1911.

The *Tattler* of Sulphur Springs High School December, 1911.

The *Tattler* of Sulphur Springs High School March, 1912.

The *Tattler* of Sulphur Springs High School May, 1912.

Course of Study Rules and Regulations for the Public Schools of Sulphur Springs Independent School District, 1914–1915.

Websites

Ancestry.com

Answers.com

Antiqbook

Davecol8.Tripod.com

FamilySearch.org

Findagrave.com/Sulphur Springs city cemetery

Gardner, Tennessee.utm.edu

IBDB.cominternetbroadway database

Lonestarfootball.net/Football scores 1913

Tidewatertimes.com

Titushistory.com/school

Wikipedia. Org/Wiki

Other

Alma Caldwell 1913–1914 magazine clipping scrap book

Birthright by Hargrave, Hopkins County, June Tuck

Diary of Alma Weeks Caldwell 1913–1914

Hopkins County Genealogical Society, Sulphur Springs, Texas

Statement Relative to the Service of C. E. Birthright by authority of the Secretary of Army, October, 1948

Pearce, John. *Sulphur Springs Wildcat Official Football History* 1911–1955.

The Caldwell-Thornton-Pearce-Seay family history, newspaper clippings and pictures, Sugar Land, Texas

Index

Numbers in italics indicate a picture on that page.

CPSIA information can be obtained
at www.ICGtesting.com
Printed in the USA
FFOW05n1010180914

9 781933 337616